Defining
MOMENTS

_____ ๑ ๛ _____

When *Choices* Matter Most

----- ๑ ๛ --

Defining
MOMENTS

When *Choices* Matter Most

Dan Schaeffer

DISCOVERY HOUSE
PUBLISHERS®

Discovery House Publishers is affiliated with
RBC Ministries, Grand Rapids, Michigan 49512.

Discovery House books are distributed to the trade exclusively by
Barbour Publishing, Inc., Uhrichsville, Ohio 44683.

Requests for permission to quote from this book should be directed to:
Permissions Department, Discovery House Publishers, P.O. 3566,
Grand Rapids, MI 49501.

Library of Congress Cataloging-in-Publication Data

Schaeffer, Daniel, 1958—
    Defining moments : when temptation and opportunity merge
/ by Daniel Schaeffer.
        p. cm.
    Includes bibliographical references.
    ISBN 0-57293-001-2
    1. Christian life--Biblical teaching. 2. Spiritual life--
Biblical teaching. I. Title

  BS680.C47 S34 2000
  241.—dc21

                                                        00-024066

Printed in the United States of America.

08 09 10 11 12 13 / DP / 9 8 7 6 5 4

TABLE OF CONTENTS

This book is dedicated to
Phil, Keri, and Dan Graper,
who in their greatest defining moment
became my heroes.

And to Brian,
who is now and forever
enjoying the fruit of his
eternal defining moment.

To God be the glory!

ARE YOU READY?

Defining moments! One morning you wake up, totally unaware that today you will make a decision that will define your life for years to come, perhaps forever. If you had known this moment was approaching, you would have prepared for it. But you didn't.

Such moments will cast us in either a positive or negative light. We can be defined as much by noble actions and words as by tragic ones. George Washington was defined as much by his valor and fortitude at Valley Forge as Napoleon was by his overreaching ego at Waterloo.

Each of us will experience moments that are far more important than all the others. In these moments we will say or do something because such behavior has become second nature to us. But the consequences will be drastically different. This one act may become a permanent snapshot of our lives that we will be unable to erase. When others look at us, that action, those words, that one moment, will dominate their thoughts. It will become our defining moment.

That moment is coming—maybe today, perhaps in a week, a month, or a year, but it is coming, and you won't be able to escape it. Right now you are cultivating habits and thoughts that will lead you inexorably to that moment. When it comes you will act as you have many times before, only this time, the consequences will be magnified. You can hope you will say or do the right thing, or you can prepare for that moment now.

Senator Dan Coates said, "Character cannot be summoned at the moment of crisis if it has been squandered by years of compromise and rationalization. The only testing ground for the heroic is the mundane. The only preparation for that one profound decision which can change a life, or even a nation, is those hundreds of half-conscious, self-defining, seemingly insignificant decisions made in private. Habit is the daily battleground of character."[1]

Our character is the scene of great battles. In the last analysis, it will nudge us in one direction or another. Fortunately, we can learn from those who have gone before us. The Bible is full of defining moments, both good and bad. Real people in real-life situations, just like us. From their examples we can learn how to prepare for our own defining moments.

Are you ready? In the following pages you will meet people who weren't ready for their moment, and you will see the terrible tragedy that ensued. But you will also meet those who were ready, and you will learn why.

In each case you will see yourself, for most of us embrace wise principles for living as well as habits that are unwise. These two are in constant conflict within us, each vying for privileged status. In that pivotal moment, we will choose between the two, and our lot will be irretrievably cast.

---

[1] *Reader's Digest*, Points to Ponder, June 1996, Senator Dan Coates, from *Imprimis*.

C. S. Lewis wrote, "Every time you make a choice you are turning the central part of you, the part of you that chooses, into something a little different from what it was before. And taking your life as a whole, with all your innumerable choices, all your life long you are slowly turning this central thing either into a heavenly creature or into a hellish creature; either into a creature that is in harmony with God, and with other creatures, and with itself, or else into one that is in a state of war and hatred with God, and with its fellow-creatures, and with itself."[2]

Are *you* ready?

---

[2]C. S. Lewis, *Mere Christianity*, (New York, NY: Macmillan Publishing Co., Inc., 1952), 86.

HANNAH'S STORY

Now there was a certain man from Ramathaim-zophim from the hill country of Ephraim, and his name was Elkanah the son of Jeroham, the son of Elihu, the son of Tohu, the son of Zuph, an Ephraimite. And he had two wives: the name of one was Hannah and the name of the other Peninnah; and Peninnah had children, but Hannah had no children.

Now this man would go up from his city yearly to worship and to sacrifice to the LORD of hosts in Shiloh. And the two sons of Eli, Hophni and Phinehas were priests to the LORD there. And when the day came that Elkanah sacrificed, he would give portions to Peninnah his wife and to all her sons and her daughters; but to Hannah he would give a double portion, for he loved Hannah, but the LORD had closed her womb. Her rival, however, would provoke her bitterly to irritate her, because the LORD had closed her womb. And it happened year after year, as often as she went up to the house of the LORD, she would provoke her, so she wept and would not eat. Then Elkanah her husband said to her, "Hannah, why do you weep and why do you not eat and why is your heart sad? Am I not better to you than ten sons?"

Then Hannah rose after eating and drinking in Shiloh. Now Eli the priest was sitting on the seat by the doorpost of the temple

of the LORD. And she, greatly distressed, prayed to the LORD and wept bitterly. And she made a vow and said, "O LORD of hosts, if Thou wilt indeed look on the affliction of Thy maidservant and remember me, and not forget Thy maidservant, but wilt give Thy maidservant a son, then I will give him to the LORD all the days of his life, and a razor shall never come on his head."

Now it came about, as she continued praying before the LORD, that Eli was watching her mouth. As for Hannah, she was speaking in her heart, only her lips were moving, but her voice was not heard. So Eli thought she was drunk. Then Eli said to her, "How long will you make yourself drunk? Put away your wine from you." But Hannah answered and said, "No, my lord, I am a woman oppressed in spirit; I have drunk neither wine nor strong drink, but I have poured out my soul before the LORD. Do not consider your maidservant as a worthless woman; for I have spoken until now out of my great concern and provocation." Then Eli answered and said, "Go in peace; and may the God of Israel grant your petition that you have asked of Him." And she said, "Let your maidservant find favor in your sight." So the woman went her way and ate, and her face was no longer sad.

Then they arose early in the morning and worshiped before the LORD, and returned again to their house in Ramah. And Elkanah had relations with Hannah his wife, and the LORD remembered her. And it came about in due time, after Hannah had conceived, that she gave birth to a son; and she named him Samuel, saying, "Because I have asked him of the LORD."

Then the man Elkanah went up with all his household to offer to the LORD the yearly sacrifice and pay his vow. But Hannah did not go up, for she said to her husband, "I will not go up until the child is weaned; then I will bring him, that he may appear before the LORD and stay there forever." And Elkanah her husband said to her, "Do what seems best to you. Remain until you have weaned him; only may the LORD confirm His word."

So the woman remained and nursed her son until she weaned him. Now when she had weaned him, she took him up with her, with a three-year-old bull and one ephah of flour and a jug of wine, and brought him to the house of the LORD in Shiloh, although the child was young. Then they slaughtered the bull, and brought the boy to Eli. And she said, "Oh, my lord! As your soul lives, my lord, I am the woman who stood here beside you, praying to the LORD. For this boy I prayed, and the Lord has given me my petition which I asked of Him. So I have also dedicated him to the Lord; as long as he lives he is dedicated to the LORD." And he worshiped the LORD there.

Then Hannah prayed and said, "My heart exults in the LORD; my horn is exalted in the LORD, My mouth speaks boldly against my enemies, because I rejoice in Thy salvation. There is no one holy like the LORD, indeed, there is no one besides Thee, nor is there any rock like our God. Boast no more so very proudly, do not let arrogance come out of your mouth; for the LORD is a God of knowledge, and with Him actions are weighed. The bows of the mighty are shattered, but the feeble gird on strength. Those who were full hire themselves out for bread, but those who were hungry cease to hunger. Even the barren gives birth to seven, but she who has many children languishes. The LORD kills and makes alive; He brings down to Sheol and raises up. The LORD makes poor and rich; He brings low, He also exalts. He raises the poor from the dust, He lifts the needy from the ash heap to make them sit with nobles, and inherit a

seat of honor; for the pillars of the earth are the LORD's, and He set the world on them. He keeps the feet of His godly ones, but the wicked ones are silenced in darkness; for not by might shall a man prevail. Those who contend with the LORD will be shattered; against them He will thunder in the heavens, the LORD will judge the ends of the earth; and He will give strength to His king, and will exalt the horn of His anointed."

1 Samuel 1:1–2:10

Now Samuel was ministering before the LORD, as a boy wearing a linen ephod. And his mother would make him a little robe and bring it to him from year to year when she would come up with her husband to offer the yearly sacrifice. Then Eli would bless Elkanah and his wife and say, "May the LORD give you children from this woman in place of the one she dedicated to the LORD." And they went to their own home. And the LORD visited Hannah; and she conceived and gave birth to three sons and two daughters. And the boy Samuel grew before the LORD.

1 Samuel 2:18–21

Chapter One

ON THE EDGE OF FULFILLMENT

The movie *Apollo 13* tells the story of that spacecraft's ill-fated mission to the moon. Mid-flight, the trip was suddenly cut short because of serious mechanical problems. The crew's perilous attempt to get home makes for compelling viewing.

One of my favorite parts of the movie is the story of Ken Mattingly, an astronaut who was originally slated to take part in the mission. At the last minute Ken was scratched from the launch due to the fear that he had contracted measles. The mission he had worked so hard and long to be a part of was to go on without him. While the others would fly into space and fame, he would remain at home. The actor accurately portrays the agony and frustration of a dream that went unfulfilled.

Yet when the Apollo 13 capsule broke down in space, it was Ken Mattingly, left behind seemingly by fate, who solved the electrical prob-

lem essential to start the computers and get the crew home safely. In the final scene, the look of satisfaction on Ken's face reminds us that this was a defining moment for him, yet one he had not envisioned. This mission was appropriately dubbed "a successful failure."

We may experience our most defining moment in the midst of a great desire or heartrending struggle. Perhaps you were spurned by someone you had a crush on in school, or you didn't make the team. Maybe you think you've missed out on marrying the man or woman of your dreams, or you're still single when you want to be married. You may not have the career you've dreamed of. In these moments and others like them, our faithfulness to God will be severely tested because the thing we want most in life, God hasn't given us—and we know that He can.

So many defining moments emerge when we are on the edge of fulfillment and yet are denied the thing we want most. These trials determine whether we can become "successful failures."

This is what makes Hannah one of my heroes. She is a familiar Sunday-school character, perhaps too familiar. The power of her story gets lost in its apparent simplicity. But there was nothing simple about Hannah—or her defining moment.

On the edge of desire

One of the great mistakes we make is in assuming that we are the only one who has an unfulfilled desire. When we see others with the very thing we long for and dream of, we feel cheated. It doesn't seem fair that someone else should get so easily what we want so desperately. Yet, have you ever considered that what you want is often not a great passion for someone who has it? His or her heart's desire is something completely different.

How ironic that though we are blessed in one way, we sense a lack of blessing in other ways! A single person who is financially successful desires most to be married. And one who is married may want more than anything else to be financially successful. The straight-A student wishes he were more athletic, while the gifted athlete wishes she were a better student. The attractive person wishes he were more relationally secure, yet the friendly person wishes she were more attractive. Each of us is blessed in different areas, and each of us is unfulfilled in different areas. The experience of unfulfillment is universal, regardless of our social standing, financial situation, or marital status.

In Hannah's case, she had the absolute devotion of her husband Elkanah. Elkanah's second wife, Peninnah, understood she was second fiddle. But Peninnah could give children to Elkanah to carry on his name—a matter of crucial importance in the Hebrew culture. Hannah, on the other hand, could not.

It was common in that culture for a man to marry one woman for love and then, if she remained barren, to take another wife to bear his children. This was Hannah's pain—no children to love, no children to care for, no heir to give to the husband she loved. To make matters worse, Peninnah had not one child but many. Hannah was bleeding from multiple wounds.

Yet God had not withheld blessing from Hannah. When Hannah was in her deepest despair about being childless, her tenderhearted, devoted husband displayed the depth of his love for her. He gave her a double portion of the sacrificial meal as if to say, "I love you twice as much, even without children. I love you for you, Hannah, not for the children you can give me."

Most women would be overjoyed to have a husband so devoted to them, so tender and compassionate. Certainly Hannah was grateful for this. But she wanted a child. Until she had one, she would feel unfulfilled.

Witnessing Elkanah's tenderness toward Hannah prompted jealousy in Peninnah. So she struck Hannah where it hurt the most—she taunted her for her inability to conceive. Although Hannah never retaliated in kind, how she must have dreaded going to the temple, for it exposed her deepest wounds! Few things are more painful than knowing God can remove our pain and fulfill our dream, but He chooses not to do so.

Was Hannah the only one with unfulfilled desires? No! Peninnah surely wanted Elkanah's devotion and love as much as Hannah wanted children. Our world is full of people who feel inadequate and incomplete. They're chasing an elusive dream. Our attitude in these moments is what will truly define us. We are tempted to blame or abandon God. But this is precisely where Hannah shines so brightly, and why the Holy Spirit chose her story for our encouragement.

Unfulfillment is not God's punishment

An unfulfilled desire can feel like a punishment. It's as if God has grounded us. Hannah must have struggled with this. In her Hebrew culture, barrenness was seen as a sign of personal failure and even as the punishment of God. When her family went to the tabernacle to give their peace offerings, a portion of the meat was given to each family member. Hannah had to sit and watch as Elkanah gave a portion to Peninnah and to each of her children. It was a constant reminder to Hannah of her perceived inadequacies as a woman, as a wife.

Are you feeling pangs of unfulfillment? Are you lacking what someone else has? Do you feel that somehow God is punishing you? If you are in continual financial distress or have seen others advancing in their careers while you stagnate; if you have never married, or you've had an unfaithful spouse; if you, like Hannah, are unable to have children, you might be tempted to assume it is God's punishment. The more acutely we feel the pain of our inadequacy, the greater will be our temptation to accuse God of unfairness and withhold our worship. These human tendencies make Hannah's actions all the more commendable.

Peninnah provides a stark contrast to Hannah's attitude. She seems to have concluded that her children were a personal accomplishment and not the blessing of the Lord. As she tormented Hannah over her predicament, Peninnah flaunted her own favorable situation and treated God's blessing as a personal triumph. Her taunts insinuated that she thought she was more loved by God than was Hannah.

Hannah understood that her dilemma was not God's punishment. We know this because of her prayer at the temple. She did not confess any sin to God but simply asked Him to give her what He had withheld. It was an uncomplicated, honest prayer. In it we clearly see Hannah's faith shining through, and we learn four valuable principles for similar moments in our own lives. First, we learn that we must:

Be willing to pray for a desire God may never fulfill

In verse eleven Hannah prayed an extraordinary prayer. She told God, "If Thou wilt . . . give Thy maidservant a son, then I will give him to the Lord all the days of his life, and a razor shall never come on his head."

It is difficult to appreciate fully what Hannah was promising. Hannah was preparing to give up the very thing she most wanted! If God would give her a son, Hannah promised to dedicate him as a Nazirite for life.

Hebrew women traditionally weaned their children at the age of three. This meant that Hannah would give up her three-year-old son forever if God would bless her with a male child.

She wasn't making a deal with God—"If you do this, then I'll do that." Hannah was committed to glorifying God with anything He gave her, including a son. She recognized that since it would take a supernatural act of God for her to have a child, God's purpose for such a child must be special. Isn't this precisely what God had in mind after all? But Hannah didn't make the commitment flippantly.

Have you ever had a three-year-old? I have, and it is one of my favorite times in their lives. At the age of three, my son found a black pen, and with his diaper as his only clothing proceeded to indulge his artistic flair on his stomach, legs, and arms. I can still remember him on the stairs, proudly displaying his "body art," grinning mischievously—and it endeared him to me all the more. Also at three, my eldest daughter Christi caught her first fish on her tiny Mickey Mouse pole. She couldn't wait to show Mommy. I lived for moments like those. My youngest, Katie, when she was three, would turn on the stereo and beg me to watch her dance

about the living room. When I applauded at the end, she wanted to do it again and again, and so did I. Never did I enjoy my children more.

Yet three years of age is when Hannah would have to give up her son, with no promise she would ever have another child. It's one thing to promise the unknown, quite another to let go of "Sammy," who might try to cling to you when you leave and reach out for Mommy with tears in his eyes. A simple story can get a lot more complicated, can't it?

This is what is so amazing about Hannah. In her most defining moment, after praying for a son that she must have prayed for hundreds of times before, at her lowest point, almost despairing, what does she do? She goes again to God. Just because He hasn't acted yet does not mean He won't.

No fuzzy prayers

Hannah did not offer up the kind of fuzzy prayers we so often do: "Help me God in my need." She wanted a baby, a son who would remove her shame and feelings of inadequacy and incompleteness. She wanted to hug and love and nurse her own child, to laugh and play with him and care for him. She wanted this so much it was tearing her up inside.

If we pray for a million dollars, or for someone else's husband or wife, or instant beauty or talent transformation, we are committing the sin James derided so strongly. "You ask and do not receive, because you ask with wrong motives, so that you may spend it on your pleasures" (James 4:3). Our motivation in these prayers is not the glory of God, but luxury and pleasure. But the natural desire of a married woman is a child; there is nothing sinful in that prayer. We're often afraid to pray too specifically because we leave ourselves open to disappointment. God may say "No." But in Hannah's defining moment she was willing to receive "No."

She gave God the option of saying no and still being her God, still being the One she would worship. Can you pray in the same way?

"Lord, "I pray with all my heart for _____, but if I don't get it, You will still be my God, and I will still love and serve you."

What if God had not given Hannah the answer she wanted? Would she have remained faithful? Yes, she would have! How do we know? Because that's exactly what had been happening year after year. Yearly she had asked the same thing and every year God said "No." Yet she returned again and again, her faith strong enough to believe He could do this thing for her, her love for Him strong enough to accept a "no."

A strong faith carried Hannah in her darkest days. Even when she failed to get her request, she did not blame God.

The second principle Hannah teaches us is that we must:

Never give God an ultimatum

Hannah never gave God an ultimatum, either consciously or unwittingly. Notice in her prayer she said, "*If thou wilt ...*" (emphasis added). She recognized that God was under no obligation to provide her with a son. He would still be a God of love, mercy, and righteousness even if she did not receive her deepest desire.

Though Hannah still had no baby, nor even a promise of one, her appetite returned and she was encouraged. Eli offered only a general prayer, requesting God to bless her with children. It was hardly a prophecy. Hannah's faith had been strengthened by the smallest token, and she again put her life in God's hand to do with as He would.

Sometimes that's when our greatest peace comes—not when we get what we most want, but when we finally and completely place the issue in God's care and are fully prepared to accept any answer He may give.

When we place God under an obligation to give us what we most desire, we create a situation in which God must become our servant. We treat Him as our personal Santa Claus, who exists to serve our every wish and whim so long as we're "good." Hannah didn't do that. She treated God always as her sovereign Lord whom she would love and serve whole-heartedly, with or without a child.

The third lesson we learn from Hannah's life is this:

Let nothing come between yourself and God

When God doesn't answer our prayers in the time or way that we want, we tend to move away from Him in disappointment. We may ultimately learn to accept the answer to our prayer, but often a cynicism sets in. We stop asking God for anything important. A subtle wound develops in our relationship with Him. We conclude that He does not really have our best at heart. Disappointment becomes the sand in the engine of our souls.

Hannah's unfulfilled desire, which was a daily burden, drew her closer to God. Look again at 1 Samuel 1:10. "And she, greatly distressed, prayed to the LORD and wept bitterly." Hannah simply did that which she had been in the habit of doing. This prepared her for her defining moment. She resisted the urge to trade her devotion to God for an aching desire. She refused to grow bitter toward the Lord, though she must have been sorely tempted to do so. When she prayed and asked God for her answer to prayer and He remained silent, she drew nearer to Him, not further away.

Years ago, a youth pastor at a church I attended was caught in an immoral situation with a member of the youth group. It was devastating for the church, the youth pastor, and his family. But as we talked with the man, who had served the Lord faithfully for years, a painful story emerged. In a moment of tears and transparency, he shared how years earlier he had gone into the ministry and had been encouraged by those around him. They told him that he was "going places" in his work for God. This expectation became a cancer in his heart. Although his ministry was by every account successful, one day he realized that he wasn't going to attain the level of success he had expected. His ministry, though genuine in many respects, had been tainted with selfish ambition in the belief that somewhere down the road there was a payoff.

This youth minister's relationship with God had drifted from a true loving servant-relationship to a business/customer relationship. When he realized he had spent so many years working for something that wasn't going to come about, he became disillusioned, and his relationship with God suffered. His defection wasn't sudden, it was a slow, gradual shifting of focus. Disappointment with God had eroded his devotion to Him.

In contrast, this is where Hannah is such a shining example. Hidden deep within her soul was the key to her greatest defining moment—she allowed nothing to come between her and God.

Hannah's faithfulness to God would not go unrewarded—and neither will yours. This does not mean you will get everything you desperately want. It may mean that He will change your heart's desire rather than fulfill it—but you will bless Him for doing so.

Fourthly, and above all else:

Love God more than you love personal desire

This is the cause of Hannah's remarkable defining moment—she loved God even more than she loved Samuel. This love led to the ultimate act of trust, something that could never have been accomplished otherwise. Do not hurry past this lesson—linger, and ponder it carefully.

In chapter two, we read Hannah's prayer of thanksgiving. We cannot fully appreciate this song of praise from Hannah until we remember that she spoke these words before she had any other children, and after she had given up her baby to Eli. Having just left her precious son in Eli's hands, having just given away the most precious possession she had, she wrote this praise to God.

Hannah's love for God was greater than her love for the gifts He gave her. That is why this is such a marvelous and touching defining moment.

I remember one young woman in a singles group I pastored years ago. She had led an immoral lifestyle, but I had the opportunity of leading her to Christ. Her conversion was complete and transforming.

Her most obvious asset was her striking beauty. In the past she had used it selfishly, to satisfy her own desires. However, when she became a Christian she began to use that gift and dedicate it to God. She attracted

men the way dogs attract fleas, but instead of abusing the gift God had given her, she used it for Him. She was continually bringing men to our group, several of whom later accepted Christ. She never led them on, nor acted inappropriately toward them, but since they wanted to be where she was, she went to church and they followed. She had surrendered her whole being to Christ, and He used it to glorify Himself.

What helped Hannah make the right choice in her defining moment? It was very simply her love for God. It is only when we love God that we are able to accept any answer from Him in regard to the things we pray for.

Right now you may be on the very edge of fulfillment or unfulfillment. You are not alone. Unfulfillment is part and parcel of life. Heaven is the only place where every desire will be totally fulfilled.

Being without something you desperately want is not God's punishment. In fact, it may be His blessing. Are you willing to pray for a desire God may choose never to fulfill, and still consider Him worthy of your love and worship? Will you refuse the temptation to place Him under an obligation to meet your every whim? If you can keep your unfulfilled desire from coming between you and the Lord, you will be demonstrating that you love God even more than your own desire. This is the ultimate act of worship, and the perfect prelude to your grandest hour.

DISCUSSION QUESTIONS

Read 1 Samuel 1:1–2:21

1. On a scale of 1-10, ten being highest, where would you place yourself in terms of your own fulfilled desire?

   1—2—3—4—5—6—7—8—9—10

2. If you feel free to share, what is the main source of unfulfillment in your life at present?

3. In which areas of your life do you feel most fulfilled? Compare your areas of fulfillment with others in your group. Are some weak where others are strong? What spiritual lesson can you draw from this?

4. Although Hannah was unfulfilled by not having children, God still blessed her through her husband's devotion. In spite of your own unfulfillment, how has God blessed you? (List at least 3 major areas. Ask others in the group to help you).

5. Can being unfulfilled feel like punishment from God, and yet not be? What other purpose could God have through your unfulfillment?

6. When you don't immediately get the answer to your prayers, are you tempted to stop praying, or to stop praying for the specific issue you feel the strongest about? Why do you think this might happen, and what does it reveal about our attitude towards God?

7. It was stated that disappointment is "sand in the engine of our souls." If God doesn't give us what we want, we tend to move away from Him in disappointment. How could you use that same unfulfilled desire to draw closer to God, as Hannah did?

Personal Reflection

Unfulfillment is part and parcel of our existence. The only place we will be totally fulfilled is in heaven. You may not receive the answer to some of your most heartfelt desires, but how that affects your relationship to God is up to you. Jesus prayed in the Garden of Gethsemane that He wouldn't have to go to the cross. He didn't want to go, yet He did. The question is: Can we still love, trust, and serve God with our whole heart, even if He doesn't give us what we most desire? Has our desire for a certain thing become an ultimatum to God, "Serve me, or I'll leave you"?

Follow-through

Write down your greatest area of unfulfillment. Ask God to strengthen your faith and give you wisdom as you commit to the following prayer.

"Lord, I pray with all my heart for _____, but if I don't receive it, You will still be my God, and I will still love and serve You. I ask only that You grant me the grace to trust that you have a different plan for my life, and that Your love for me is greater than ever."

THE STORY OF LOT

So Abram went up from Egypt to the Negev, he and his wife and all that belonged to him; and Lot with him. Now Abram was very rich in livestock, in silver and in gold. And he went on his journeys from the Negev as far as Bethel, to the place where his tent had been at the beginning, between Bethel and Ai, to the place of the altar, which he had made there formerly; and there Abram called on the name of the LORD.

Now Lot, who went with Abram, also had flocks and herds and tents. And the land could not sustain them while dwelling together; for their possessions were so great that they were not able to remain together. And there was strife between the herdsmen of Abram's livestock and the herdsmen of Lot's livestock. Now the Canaanite and the Perizzite were dwelling then in the land. Then Abram said to Lot, "Please let there be no strife between you and me, nor between my herdsmen and your herdsmen, for we are brothers. Is not the whole land before you? Please separate from me: if to the left, then I will go to the right; or if to the right, then I will go to the left."

And Lot lifted up his eyes and saw all the valley of the Jordan, that it was well watered everywhere—this was before the LORD destroyed Sodom and Gomorrah—like the garden of the LORD, like the land of Egypt as you go to Zoar. So Lot chose for him-

self all the valley of the Jordan; and Lot journeyed eastward. Thus they separated from each other. Abram settled in the land of Canaan, while Lot settled in the cities of the valley, and moved his tents as far as Sodom. Now the men of Sodom were wicked exceedingly and sinners against the Lord.

Genesis 13:1–13

But he hesitated. So the men seized his hand and the hand of his wife and the hands of his two daughters, for the compassion of the Lord was upon him; and they brought him out, and put him outside the city. And it came about when they had brought them outside, that one said, "Escape for your life! Do not look behind you, and do not stay anywhere in the valley; escape to the mountains, lest you be swept away."

But Lot said to them, "Oh no, my lords! Now behold, your servant has found favor in your sight, and you have magnified your lovingkindness, which you have shown me by saving my life; but I cannot escape to the mountains, lest the disaster overtake me and I die; now behold, this town is near enough to flee to, and it is small. Please, let me escape there (is it not small?) that my life may be saved." And he said to him, "Behold, I grant you this request also, not to overthrow the town of which you have spoken. Hurry, escape there, for I cannot do anything until you arrive there." Therefore the name of the town was called Zoar.

The sun had risen over the earth when Lot came to Zoar. Then the LORD rained on Sodom and Gomorrah brimstone and fire from the Lord out of heaven, and He overthrew those cities, and all the valley, and all the inhabitants of the cities, and what grew on the ground. But his wife, from behind him, looked back; and she became a pillar of salt.

Genesis 19:16–26

Chapter Two

THE TRAGIC TALE
OF AN EMPTY LOT

There is a windy mountain road leading up to the High Sierra Mountains on the way to Yosemite National Park. The road passes through several small towns and an occasional home or small business. When I first started making that drive I recall seeing a large steak house that had closed recently. "For Sale" signs were everywhere, along with the name of the restaurant. The building was still in good repair, nicely painted, and pleasant to look at. I wondered what restaurant would be there the next time I came through.

It has been sixteen years, and that building is still empty. The paint is old and faded, the windows boarded up, the parking lot overgrown with weeds. When this restaurant first opened it must have bustled with activity, plates, silverware, and glasses clinking, wait-staff scurrying to get food, music playing, people talking, laughing, and socializing. I've often wondered what caused it to close its doors.

This restaurant had been someone's dream. But now the dream has died. The building stands vacant and lonely. No one goes there except for the occasional vagrant looking for shelter. It is a sad picture. It is also the tragic story of many people's lives.

In this chapter, we will look at the true-life story of a real empty Lot. His story is found in Genesis chapters 13, 14, and 19. Lot was the nephew of Abram, whom the Lord later called Abraham, the father of the Jewish race. Here we read about Lot's defining decision—the decision that so mirrored his whole life and set the tone for the rest of it.

Both Abram and Lot were wealthy men who resided in a foreign country. It was a land that belonged to the Canaanites and the Perizzites. The area where Abram and Lot were living could no longer support two great herds of animals. With no fences or borders to determine where one's grazing rights began and another's ended, the herdsmen of the two relatives began to fight. So Abram stepped in and made a wise decision. There was enough room for both of them if they went in different directions.

Abram was the patriarch of the two, and the one to whom God had promised all this land (Genesis 12:6–7). As the proper recipient of the entire region, Abram could have chosen the land he wanted and left the rest to Lot. But Abram showed his godliness by trusting God to keep His promise in His own way. He graciously allowed Lot to choose which land he wanted.

Humanly speaking, it wasn't a hard decision for Lot. The Jordan Valley was a lush green place, and Sodom and Gomorrah were beautiful and desirable places to live. Lot didn't think twice. He saw the fertile land of the plains and chose it.

While this decision seemed shrewd for Lot, it turned out badly. His shallow choice reflected his true character, and revealed him to be, in several ways, an empty Lot.

Through Lot's life we can discern four dangers to beware of when making defining-moment decisions—four dangers that will keep you from becoming an empty Lot yourself. The first danger is:

The danger of deceiving yourself

From Lot's tragic life we learn that there are no harmless character flaws. When we read chapter 13:10–13, it is clear that self-interest and greed drove Lot's decision. Although Abram could rightfully have chosen where he would live, he humbled himself and allowed Lot to choose. Furthermore, Abram initiated the solution to the problem.

Significantly, the Bible does call Lot a righteous man. In 2 Peter 2:6–8, Peter reminds us that God "condemned the cities of Sodom and Gomorrah to destruction by reducing them to ashes, having made them an example to those who would live ungodly lives thereafter; and if He rescued righteous Lot, oppressed by the sensual conduct of unprincipled men (for by what he saw and heard that righteous man, while living among them, felt his righteous soul tormented day after day with their lawless deeds)."

Lot was a righteous man because he believed God, expressed his faith in God, and did not approve of the horrible sins of Sodom and Gomorrah. In this passage, however, it seems that Lot's righteousness is contrasted not with Abram's but with that of the citizens of Sodom and Gomorrah. It is possible to appear to be morally upstanding but have one or two tragic character flaws that eventually surface.

One of Lot's flaws was that he struggled with selfishness. He desired the best of the land for himself, and he was in a position to get it. Sodom and Gomorrah were wealthy enclaves, places of great riches because of the fertileness of the region. People like to live in beautiful places, and usually only the wealthiest can afford to.

Lot's greed is evident in other passages as well. When God sent judgment upon Sodom and Gomorrah, we gain valuable insight into Lot's character. God had determined to obliterate the towns for their sin and unrepentance. Yet, though Lot knew this, he didn't want to leave. God sent angels in the form of men to protect Lot from the judgment. But the men of Sodom demanded that Lot hand them over so they could rape them. That is how perverse the people of Sodom had become.

In spite of this horrible decadence, Lot still didn't want to leave. The angels literally had to drag him and his family out of Sodom. The scriptural accounts says, "But he hesitated. So the men seized his hand and the hand of his wife and the hands of his two daughters, for the compassion of the Lord was upon him; and they brought him out, and put him outside the city" (Genesis 19:16).

Hesitated! Why? The reason is simple. Everything Lot had attained was about to be destroyed—all his wealth, his business contacts, his home, his job, everything but his very life. He still didn't want to give it up. You may be thinking, "But I thought he was a righteous man?" Can a person be a Christian and still have a defective character? Yes! Greed, desire, envy, and jealousy don't go away just because you become a Christian. Sooner or later, God makes us face those issues and brings them to our attention. It cost Lot everything he had before God got his attention.

Weeds

If not dealt with properly, a single weak character trait can have a negative effect on the rest of our lives. In Lot's life, greed and self-interest were present, even though he appeared to be a morally upstanding individual.

The heart of the Christian is like a garden. When we are born again, God plants His fruit, the fruit of the Spirit: love, joy, peace, patience, kindness, goodness, faithfulness, gentleness, and self-control (Galatians 5:22–23). But at the same time Satan keeps trying to replant his own garden in our heart. Character flaws are like weeds—they grow fastest when they are ignored and become increasingly difficult to pull out. We need to deal with such weeds when they first appear, because by the time we see the plants, the roots are already formed and growing.

My wife, Annette, and I planted a little garden. We planted corn, pumpkins, cantaloupe, watermelon, beans, herbs, squash, and sunflowers. We planted all those on purpose; we wanted them to grow. We watered them carefully and cultivated them. But weeds popped up without any attention whatsoever. They grew marvelously. We had to pull the weeds continually. We never tended the weeds; the more we neglected them, the better they grew.

The spiritual garden we want must be tended in order to grow, but a spiritual "weed" will flourish with inattention. What weed, or character flaw, are you ignoring? If you ignore it long enough, one day that flaw will grow so large it will be the only thing that people can see in you. All your good qualities will be hidden behind that one character flaw you have ignored.

You may be there right now. Caring people may have already discussed this flaw with you. They have seen how it has taken over your life. When you try to point out all your good qualities, they can't seem to see them. Your character flaw is now so blatant that it overshadows all your other good qualities. You may be on your way to becoming an empty Lot.

Some Christians joke about their character flaws. "That's just who I am," they will tell you with a grin. They seem to think a character flaw is just a personality trait. But the Bible never treats them that way.

I heard of a pastor who was cursing in his sermons and criticizing people he was angry with from the pulpit. He got into a fistfight with an elder at his church at a basketball game. When confronted with this sin, his excuse was "Hey, that's just me, that's my personality. It's the way I am, no big deal."

He equated his activity with a personality trait that was supposedly beyond his control. Shyness is a personality trait. Being gregarious is a personality trait. But sin is sin! And sins are weeds that must be pulled.

Don't deceive yourself. There are no harmless character flaws.

But there is a second danger to consider.

The danger of altering God's price tags
Genesis 13:10 tells us, "And Lot lifted up his eyes and saw all the valley of the Jordan, that it was well watered everywhere—this was before the Lord destroyed Sodom and Gomorrah—like the garden of the Lord, like the land of Egypt as you go to Zoar."

Everything Lot could see with his eyes looked good. He was smitten with the great lust of which John the apostle spoke in 1 John 2:16: "For all that is in the world, the lust of the flesh and the lust of the eyes and the boastful pride of life, is not from the Father, but is from the world."

One commentator points out that the Hebrew word for sin means to miss the mark, and went on to say, "So a sinner is one who is ever aiming at happiness and constantly missing his mark; because . . . he seeks for happiness where it can never be found."[1] Lot didn't look beyond what his eyes could see. He knew that Sodom was an immoral town. It's reputation was well-known. But it was an attractive place. While Lot never adopted the religion of the people of Sodom and Gomorrah, or their immoral practices, he was smitten with their culture, their "stuff." They were a people who were looking for happiness where it couldn't be found, and Lot seemed to have the same weakness.

God places the price tags in life where they belong. He tells us what is valuable and what is worthless. When God's price tags don't seem to make sense to us we are tempted to change them. Lot chose Sodom and Gomorrah, the capital cities of the "good life." The result? Lot's righteous soul was constantly offended, oppressed and influenced by the sinful lifestyle about him. In chapter 14 we read that enemies captured Lot, and Abram had to rescue him. He no doubt lived a compromised lifestyle in Sodom, one that likely contributed to the low moral standards of his daughters (see Genesis 19:30–38). He had to be rescued by angels, lost his wife, his sons-in-law, his livelihood, and barely escaped with his own life. Lot paid dearly for his poor choice.

Recently, Annette and I struck up a conversation with a clerk in our local Barnes & Noble bookstore. She seemed despondent, and mentioned that her house had recently burned down. She sadly shared how she had lost some 75,000 baseball cards she had been collecting as part of a business venture. All her plaques and honors accumulated over the years were also destroyed.

[1] *The Bethany Parallel Commentary, Old Testament,* Adam Clark, p. 45.

When I asked her if anyone was hurt, she nonchalantly shook her head no, as if the question were ultimately unimportant and she derived no comfort from it. Her stuff was of great value to her. They were destroyed in much the same way Lot's things were, by fire. Bible commentator F. B. Meyer wrote, "The world is full of Lots—shallow, impulsive, doomed to be revealed by their choice."[2]

Have you exchanged price tags in your life? The things we value become the basis for our most important and defining decisions. If we value money and prestige we will chase a job that brings us these things but little else. We all know scores of people unhappy in their jobs—but who are now trapped. The things that bring them fulfillment don't make them enough money, and they are too attached to their lifestyle to make the necessary changes. Work becomes a grind, and they grow miserable.

I know men and women who married their spouses primarily for their looks. This is what they valued most in a mate. But now, five, ten, fifteen years later, the luster has worn off. They wish they had married someone more understanding, thoughtful, and considerate—the qualities their spouses lack and which now cause them such pain. All around them they see couples who are physically less attractive but are fulfilled in marriage.

When we value all the status possessions of our world—bigger, more expensive homes, more expensive and newer cars—we can find ourselves sacrificing everything to get them. Spending beyond our means, we end up in debt and unable to enjoy the very possessions we have sacrificed so much to have. In these and many other decisions like them, we can find that our choices reveal who we really are.

What do your choices reveal about what you value? We see this thought developed more fully in the third danger.

---

[2] *The Bethany Parallel Commentary, Old Testament,* Adam Clark, p. 44.

The danger of long-term decisions based on temporary attractions

Lot's decision was based on what he saw, what appealed to him through his physical senses. What did Lot see when he looked at the beautiful Jordan Valley and Sodom and Gomorrah? He saw three things: beauty, wealth, and ease.

The Jordan Valley was more beautiful than the territory Lot left to Abram. It was a desirable place to live. Think of the Napa Valley in California, or the South of France, where vines and orchards grow abundantly and the countryside is picturesque.

Second, there was wealth. Ample water and pasture meant additional grazing areas and increased flocks. More flocks meant more wealth, because in the ancient East, livestock had value, not currency.

Third, Lot saw ease. It would be much easier to make a living in Sodom and Gomorrah than where Abram was going. When the water is there, the grass is in abundance, and the fruit trees are already planted, you simply don't have to work as hard. Caring for the animals is much easier.

Beauty, wealth, and ease. Lot, like so many of us, was sure that the thing he now found so attractive would always be so. People are sure their looks and youth will last, their job is secure, their talent will always be in demand.

So what happened? Let's start with the beauty of Sodom and Gomorrah. It would be utterly destroyed by a volcanic-like eruption, never to be anything but a desolate plain. And Lot's great wealth? His flocks were destroyed, his business and his customers were gone, he was blessed just to escape with his life. And what about the ease of life? With his livelihood and his home removed, Lot was destined to live in a cave.

Several years ago, there was a sensational story in the news. It concerned Della and Daryl Sutorius. Daryl Sutorius was a heart surgeon who had divorced his wife of thirty years, and through a dating service met a striking woman named Della Britteon. He saw a young, quiet, eye-catching woman, and evidently thought she would be everything his previous wife had not been.

He married her only four months after his divorce. What he didn't know was that Della was used to being married, and was not at all what she seemed. She was dangerous! Each of her previous three husbands had been lucky to escape their marriage with their lives. Della was vicious and mean, and when rejected, acted violently. Less than a year after marrying this "beauty," Dr. Sutorius wanted a divorce. He never got the chance. Della killed him with a .38-caliber revolver she had bought only two days earlier.[3]

Are you making long-term decisions based on temporary attractions? That is one of the quickest ways to become an empty Lot. But finally, above all, we come to the last danger:

The danger of assuming your decisions won't affect others

We infuse those around us with our values, especially those closest to us. Let's follow the results of Lot's decision on his family. When they were escaping Sodom and Gomorrah's judgment, the angels warned them in Genesis 19:17, "Escape for your life! Do not look behind you, and do not stay anywhere in the valley; escape to the mountains, lest you be swept away." But what happened to Lot's wife? Genesis 19:26 says, "But his wife, from behind him, looked back; and she became a pillar of salt." Don't misunderstand. The Hebrew word suggests this was not a casual backward glance. It was a long look of desire, a reluctance to leave her home and possessions.

She, like her husband, was hesitating, lingering, because she didn't really want to go. God had sent angels to save them from destruction, and she didn't want to leave Sodom. She had a severe case of the same greed that Lot had.

Lot's sons-in-law didn't take his warnings seriously and were destroyed. But what of his daughters?

---

[3] *Orange County Register*, Nation: "Social climbing woman accused of killing husband." 3/12/96.

When Sodom and Gomorrah were annihilated, Lot took his daughters and hid in caves with them. His daughters decided they wanted to have children, so they got their father drunk and slept with him. These incestuous acts resulted in the Moabites and the Ammonites, two tribes who were a perpetual thorn in the side of Abraham's descendants.

This story shocks our sensibilities. Where was their faith in God's provision? Where did Lot's daughters learn to debase themselves with such horribly immoral decisions? Think about this: how much time had Lot's daughters spent in the city Daddy picked to be their home? With whom had they grown up, and from whom had they been learning? Who was influencing them day after day, night after night? What lifestyle was their culture bombarding them with continually?

Broken models

How are our decisions affecting our loved ones? Lot's faith in God remained, but his decisions had destroyed everything he valued because he had invested his life in things of no value.

Dr. Laura Schlessinger, the radio talk-show host, related how she was once at a loss for words during her call-in show. It was a call from an 11-year-old boy that rendered her speechless. He told her he had a problem. He liked a girl at school, but there was another one who was "making eyes" at him, letting him know she liked him. Should he drop his present girlfriend to chase the new one?

Dr. Laura asked the boy, "Well, how would you feel if your daddy went off with some new lady every time one showed interest?" "He did," was his matter-of-fact reply. Since no loyalty and fidelity was modeled at home, what could Dr. Laura say?[4]

---

[4]*Orange County Register,* Accent, Column: Dr. Laura Schlessinger, "Parents, your example will leave a mark."

Our values will affect—or infect—those we love. A very enlightening project might be to poll our spouses, children, and close friends, and ask them to share what they feel we value most in life from what they witness in our lives. Warning: This is not a project for the faint of heart.

If you heed this advice, your defining moment can be a wonderful one, a moment that will positively affect your family, and everyone else. Give your own story a happy ending! Don't become an empty Lot.

To avoid becoming an empty Lot beware of these four dangers:
- Don't deceive yourself —
  There are no harmless character flaws.
- Don't change God's price tags in life.
- Don't make long-term decisions
  based on temporary attractions.
- Don't assume your decisions won't
  deeply affect others.

DISCUSSION QUESTIONS

Read Genesis 13:1–13; 19:16–26

1. Can you think of a tragic decision you have made that ultimately cost you something dear? If you feel free to share this decision, what was it? If not, can you share what you feel it cost you in general terms?

2. List two or three of your personal character flaws (ex: selfishness, greed, vanity, ego, anger, jealousy, gossip, etc.). We all have them! List them from least important and inconsequential to more important and potentially damaging.

3. How do you foresee one of these flaws in your character creating a tragic defining moment for you if left unaddressed?

4. What steps have you taken to deal with your character flaw, and what does God say about it? Do you know what God says about it? (If not, look up the word in a Bible concordance).

5. Have you ever joked about your character flaws, or tried to justify them by saying, "Well, that's just the way I am"? What is the difference between a character flaw and a personality trait?

6. Lot chose the good life in Sodom and Gomorrah because it was so much more beautiful and attractive, but his decision ultimately turned sour. Can you think of any "good-life" decisions you've made that went bad? What did you learn that you could pass on to others?

7. What are some tragic good-life decisions we might make that would negatively affect those we love?

8. With what favorite values do you wish to "infect" those whom you love? How are you going about this?

9. What flawed values may you be transferring to those you love? Whom may you be infecting?

Personal Reflection

We all have character flaws, but it is tempting to justify them or joke about them, instead of dealing with them. The longer we wait to deal with these flaws, the worse they become and the closer we are to becoming an empty Lot. Imagine your most defining moment. Will it be a result of an ignored character flaw? What might you do to prevent it? Now go do it—while there's time!

Follow-through

Write down what you believe to be your greatest character flaw. Determine to make it a daily matter of prayer. Look up Scriptures related to it, and continually ask God for His power in overcoming it. Don't expect immediate changes. Actions are the result of our heart's desires—and the heart changes slowly. But start now, and don't stop!

NAAMAN

Now Naaman, captain of the army of the king of Aram, was a great man with his master, and highly respected, because by him the LORD had given victory to Aram. The man was also a valiant warrior, but he was a leper.

Now the Arameans had gone out in bands, and had taken captive a little girl from the land of Israel; and she waited on Naaman's wife. And she said to her mistress, "I wish that my master were with the prophet who is in Samaria! Then he would cure him of his leprosy." And Naaman went in and told his master, saying, "Thus and thus spoke the girl who is from the land of Israel." Then the king of Aram said, "Go now, and I will send a letter to the king of Israel." And he departed and took with him ten talents of silver and six thousand shekels of gold and ten changes of clothes. And he brought the letter to the king of Israel, saying, "And now as this letter comes to you, behold, I have sent Naaman my servant to you, that you may cure him of his leprosy." And it came about when the king of Israel read the letter, that he tore his clothes and said, "Am I God, to kill and to make alive, that this man is sending word to me to cure a man of his leprosy? But consider now, and see how he is seeking a quarrel against me."

And it happened when Elisha the man of God heard that the king of Israel had torn his clothes, that he sent word to the king,

saying, "Why have you torn your clothes? Now let him come to me, and he shall know that there is a prophet in Israel."

So Naaman came with his horses and his chariots, and stood at the doorway of the house of Elisha. And Elisha sent a messenger to him, saying, "Go and wash in the Jordan seven times, and your flesh shall be restored to you and you shall be clean." But Naaman was furious and went away and said, "Behold, I thought, 'He will surely come out to me, and stand and call on the name of the LORD his God, and wave his hand over the place, and cure the leper.' Are not Abanah and Pharpar, the rivers of Damascus, better than all the waters of Israel? Could I not wash in them and be clean?" So he turned and went away in a rage. Then his servants came near and spoke to him and said, "My father, had the prophet told you to do some great thing, would you not have done it? How much more then, when he says to you, 'Wash, and be clean'?" So he went down and dipped himself seven times in the Jordan, according to the word of the man of God; and his flesh was restored like the flesh of a little child, and he was clean.

When he returned to the man of God with all his company, and came and stood before him, he said, "Behold now, I know that there is no God in all the earth, but in Israel; so please take a present from your servant now." But he said, "As the LORD lives, before whom I stand, I will take nothing." And he urged him to take it, but he refused. And Naaman said, "If not, please let your servant at least be given two mules' load of earth; for your servant will no more offer burnt offering nor will he sacrifice to other gods, but to the LORD. In this matter may the LORD pardon your servant: when my master goes into the house of Rimmon to worship there, and he leans on my hand and I bow myself in the house of Rimmon, when I bow myself in the house of Rimmon, the LORD pardon your servant in this matter." And he said to him, "Go in peace." So he departed from him some distance.

2 Kings 5:1–19

Chapter Three

RESCUING YOUR DECISIONS FROM PRIDE AND PREJUDICE

Among the myriad of catalysts for defining moments, few are more determinative than pride and its dark shadow, prejudice. Our "enlightened" culture prides itself on its political correctness, and believes itself to be beyond the reach of these primitive attitudes. You may even feel the same way.

Yet for all our enlightenment, we are all proud of something, no matter how bad we may feel about ourselves in other areas. Maybe we are overweight yet highly successful in business. Our one strength helps us to feel pride, to feel superior to others. Or perhaps we are not successful or popular like others but we are better educated. Our education can become our source of pride. On the other hand, others may be more intelligent or successful than we are but we excel athletically. Or we may be more creative, or musical, or artistic, or mechanically inclined than others. Each of us can find at least one source of pride in our lives; most of us can find many.

Furthermore, we are all prone to prejudice. It may not be a racial prejudice, but in some way we feel better, superior to others without any rational reason to feel that way. If you honestly search your heart long enough, you'll find both pride and prejudice. Some people think that pride is a good thing, and that most of us suffer from low self-esteem. But the Bible makes the point that pride, not low-self esteem, is man's problem.

For years psychologists have favored attempts at raising the self-esteem of violent offenders. However, a review of studies on crime and aggression in *Psychological Review* found virtually no evidence linking violence to low self-image.[1] Instead, researchers concluded that high self-esteem (pride) might be the culprit, especially when a person with an inflated ego feels threatened. Roy Baumeister of Ohio's Case Western Reserve University said, "Does anyone really think the cause of world peace would be promoted if we boosted Saddam Hussein's self-esteem?" He concluded, "Perhaps it would be better to try instilling modesty and humility."

This brings us to a fellow named Naaman, who was badly afflicted with these weaknesses. However, in an ironic plot twist, in his greatest defining moment, he made the right decision—but just barely. Naaman walked a tightwire of destiny, almost falling several times. He nearly allowed years of pride and prejudice to dictate his most defining moment. But when everything he held dear was at stake—at the last possible moment—Naaman chose wisely.

The burning question is this: What kept Naaman from making a tragic defining-moment decision? Four elements worked to point

---

[1]*Psychological Review,* February 19, 1996.

Naaman in the right direction. Two of these required a great personal change in him. The other two were inherent motivations that needed a little encouragement.

Early in the story we see the most important of these four elements. Had he stumbled here, Naaman would never have been cured of leprosy. As you read, ask yourself if you've encountered a similar situation. First of all:

Naaman listened to people he usually ignored

To understand how difficult this step was for Naaman we need to keep in mind how powerful he was. Naaman was the Norman Schwarzkopf of Aram, a great military leader and trusted confidant of the king of the Arameans. An experienced soldier and raider, he was undoubtedly fearless and bold. While that makes for a good soldier, it can create problems in other relationships.

Naaman was used to giving orders, not taking them. It is likely that the only man he had to answer to was the king himself. Yet, in God's sovereign plan, the person who pointed Naaman in the right direction was a young Jewish slave girl he had captured on one of his raids to Jewish settlements. She wasn't even a woman, she was only an unnamed girl. It is clear she wasn't ordinarily a major source of advice for him. However, she spoke to his greatest need in a way that no one else could.

Let's pause for a moment and allow this to sink in. Sometimes we come across powerful people in our lives. It may be a boss, or a respected family member, a successful businessperson, a gifted athlete, or a prominent public figure. We are often too intimidated to speak to them about Christ because they are so intimidating. But we must understand that even powerful people will listen when we address a need no one else has been able to meet.

Because of Naaman's desperate need for healing, he listened to the girl. She prompted him to visit Israel and seek out Elisha, the great prophet. Later, when Naaman met Elisha and wasn't given the VIP treatment he felt his position merited, his pride almost derailed the whole

process. But notice again who stopped him. It was his servants. Their kind, concerned, and reasonable words reached him. Can you see how God was dealing with Naaman on every level of his pride?

Naaman is not unique. His problem is a perennial one. "Pride goes before destruction, and a haughty spirit before stumbling" (Proverbs 16:18). Naaman was ready to stumble badly, but at the last moment he recovered.

Listen to the quiet voices

Ask yourself who God has put into your life to help you make the right decisions. It may be the person you are least likely to listen to or take seriously. You ignore him or her at your own peril, and could be setting yourself up to miss one of the greatest blessings of your life. God may well speak to you through some of the quiet voices you have learned to ignore.

That voice we've learned to tune out may be our spouse, our children, our parents, our employer, or simply someone God has placed in our lives for that one defining moment when we are going to receive—or lose—a tremendous blessing. That person will urge us to do what our pride and prejudices reject, and we will be sorely tempted to ignore them.

As a pastor there have been times when I have tried to convince my board of the merits of an idea of mine, something I was very excited about. But some of my ideas have been greeted with less enthusiasm than I envisioned. I have been blessed with godly and wise men on our board and have learned to swallow my pride and listen to the voice of concern. Ironically, it is usually expressed by someone quieter, who almost apologizes for his reluctance to embrace my great new idea. His was the quiet voice of wisdom, and I have never regretted following wise advice to make a change.

Without exception, Christians who have made tragic defining-moment decisions have had people warn them not to take the step they were considering. However, their pride caused them to ignore that person, and they allowed a dangerous habit to reap its bitter fruit.

No cruise-control

I frequently take long vacations with my family, which requires long drives. During those inevitable stretches of freeway where traffic is light I engage my cruise-control and move my foot away from the accelerator and brake. When I reach city traffic, however, I disengage the cruise-control. I want my foot near the accelerator and brake because dangerous situations could develop quickly, and I need to be far more cautious.

If I'm facing a decision with little ultimate importance, I can safely ignore the advice of others, such as what color car to buy, or whether to get a Big Mac or a Whopper for lunch. The consequences in either case will be mild. But for decisions with greater consequences, my need to listen to others intensifies rapidly. I must switch off my lazy mental cruise-control and be attentive to those who give me wise advice. I must listen carefully, searching for nuggets of gold from folks I've gotten used to ignoring.

Let's look at the second big step Naaman took:

Naaman restrained his pride and prejudice to step out in faith

Like an unbroken colt, pride and prejudice will not be tamed easily. It takes effort, time, and persistence with prayer, but you can harness them so that they no longer run wild and dangerous.

It's understandable that Naaman would have been tempted to indulge in a little pride and prejudice as he approached Elisha. He had been victorious over these Hebrews before, he had even taken Hebrew slaves. It would be easy for him to develop a sense of superiority. But when he arrived in Israel and went to Elisha's house he was in for a rude awakening. Elisha didn't even come out to greet him! Instead, he sent a servant to instruct Naaman to wash seven times in the Jordan.

In the ancient East there was an unwritten code based on a person's social rank that prescribed how he was to be treated and received. Naaman's social standing demanded that Elisha go out to greet him personally with great pomp and circumstance, but he didn't. It wasn't because Naaman was a leper; it was because God wanted to deal with Naaman's real problem—pride.

We can't come before God with an inflated ego. James reminds us, "God is opposed to the proud, but gives grace to the humble" (James 4:6).

In Naaman's defense, this was all new to him. In Aram, everyone but the king himself would have to bow down to him and serve his every wish in the most reverential manner. Now this Hebrew prophet and his messenger were treating him quite commonly, injuring his sense of superiority. No red carpets were being rolled out, no trumpets were sounding, just a servant telling him to go wash seven times in the Jordan River and he would be healed.

This was too much for someone accustomed to reverential treatment. Naaman was ready to ditch the whole idea, pack his bags, and go home. To make matters worse, Naaman was right. The Jordan was a dirty little river compared to the clear and beautiful rivers of Damascus. Furthermore, no explanation was given as to why he should wash seven times in the Jordan. The Jordan wasn't a magic river with special healing properties.

The answer—never explained to Naaman—was because the Jordan River was in Israel, the land of Jehovah. Why wash seven times? Because seven is the biblical number of perfection, indicating a miracle of God would take place. Who was going to heal Naaman? God was! And God insisted that Naaman accept the words of the prophet by faith.

Asking God to explain Himself

Predictably, Naaman was furious. As one wise man aptly put it, "Temper gets people into trouble. Pride keeps them there." None of Naaman's questions were answered; none of his objectives had been addressed. But God did not have to explain Himself to Naaman.

One of the many weaknesses of human nature is that we are constantly asking God to explain Himself before we will obey Him. If His explanation makes sense to us, we go along. If not, we resist. We must ask God to help us deny our own pride and prejudice and step out in faith, but that is easier said than done. Pride feeds on self-importance.

The story is told of a prosperous young stockbroker who fell in love with a rising young actress of gentility and dignity. He frequently escorted her about town and soon wanted to marry her. Concerned about his own fortune and reputation, he decided to have a private investigation service check her out. He asked the agency not to reveal his own identity to the investigator who was making the report. When the report came back, it revealed the actress had an unblemished past, a spotless reputation, and her friends and associates were of the highest caliber. The only shadow over her, the report concluded, was that she was seen around town in the company of a young stockbroker of dubious business practices and principles.

Feelings of superiority lead us to treat others as inferior. But like that stockbroker, when we think too highly about ourselves, we're in for a rude awakening.

If Naaman had refused to swallow his pride and prejudice, he would have remained a leper to the day of his death. If he had not humbly stepped out in faith toward God, he would have lost his soul as well as his life. But Naaman stepped out of character and into faith. It was not a blind leap, but it *was* a big step.

There's a third key aspect to Naaman's defining moment:

Naaman had an overwhelming desire to change

Despite his ingrained pride and prejudice, there was one thing even more compelling in his life. Naaman desperately wanted to be cured of leprosy. He jumped at the faint hope given by the Hebrew slave girl.

One of the greatest motivations we can experience is the overwhelming desire to escape something painful. The burden has become so terrible to us, so unbearable, that we are willing to consider doing something we previously would have rejected.

In Naaman's life that something was leprosy. It is a hideous disease that makes its victims repulsive to others. To a man of Naaman's accomplishments and pride, this must have been unbearable. I'm sure he had

tried every kind of religious cure he could find, and every other kind of cure before he tried God. Success and achievement produced nothing in his life that would have brought him to seek God and find healing.

Have you noticed that there are phases in people's lives when they aren't open to hearing about their need for God and forgiveness and salvation? We speak to them, but they won't hear us. Then, inexplicably, something comes into their life that they can't handle. Maybe it's an addiction, or purposelessness, or a threat to a precious relationship, but eventually they realize that they can't solve the problem themselves. They come to the point where God wants them to be—to the end of their human resources and solutions. They can't fix it, they can't make it better, they can't make it go away. Nothing but a miracle can save them. It is here, at their lowest point, that they are closer to God than they have ever been. Finally, their pride is broken.

My wife and I have some very close friends who share a wonderful testimony that illustrates the transforming power of Christ. They were both Christians when they got married, but the husband soon became abusive and domineering. His wife grew to fear him. She prayed for him, and others spoke to him, but to no avail. The situation got worse, until finally the husband came down with a serious illness. Sick, discouraged, and broken, he repented of his sinful attitudes and actions toward his wife and rededicated his life to Christ. Today they have a wonderful marriage. He dotes on her, and she loves him wholeheartedly. Life had become so miserable that he was finally willing to do whatever was necessary to change. God had to plant within his heart a desire for change, and the seed He used was illness.

The overwhelming desire to change his condition helped Naaman make a decision he otherwise would not have considered. The seeds for a much-needed change may be present in you as well. Don't ignore them. God is using them to get your attention.

Leprosy!

Did Naaman's leprosy actually keep him from making a tragic decision? Absolutely. His leprosy was the means of his humiliation. Without a willingness to humble himself before both men and God, Naaman would have been neither healed nor saved. His leprosy brought him to see his need for God, exactly the purpose for which God designed it. Naaman's desire to be healed forced him to admit that everything he had believed before about Israel and God, and about himself, was wrong. It's unlikely he would have arrived at this conclusion without the disease.

Why does God allow us to go through painful and tragic events? Because pain plants the flag of reality in the heart of a rebel fortress. "Pain," C. S. Lewis observed, "is God's megaphone" to rouse a deaf world to the true realities of life. Ironically, only pain and suffering do that. Success, pleasure, and ease produce pride and prejudice—not humility. The things we pursue and view as blessings are often curses.

Naaman had a progressively deteriorating condition which would have destroyed him—he also had leprosy. Would Naaman have ever gone to see Elisha if he hadn't had leprosy? No! Would he have ever humbled himself except to get rid of this hated disease? No! Then was his leprosy a curse? No, it was the means to his healing, and more importantly, his salvation.

The school of hard knocks

In Gary Richmond's wonderful book, *A View from the Zoo*, he tells about the birth of a giraffe. He writes, "The first things to emerge are the baby giraffe's front hooves and head. A few minutes later the plucky newborn calf is hurled forth, falls ten feet, and lands on its back. Within seconds, he rolls to an upright position with is legs tucked under his body. The mother giraffe lowers her head long enough to take a quick look. Then she positions herself directly over her calf. She waits for about a minute, and then she does the most unreasonable thing. She swings her long, pendulous leg outward and kicks her baby, so that it is sent sprawling head over heels. When it doesn't get up, the violent process is repeated again and again. The struggle to rise is momentous. As the baby calf grows tired, the mother kicks it again to stimulate its efforts. Finally the calf stands for the first time on its wobbly legs. Then the mother giraffe does the most remarkable thing. She kicks it off its feet again. Why? She wants it to remember how it got up.

"In the wild, baby giraffes must be able to get up as quickly as possible to stay with the herd where there is safety. Lions, hyenas, leopards, and wild dogs all eat young giraffes. If the mother giraffe didn't teach her calf to get up quickly, her baby would soon be lunch.

"I can see the parallel in my own life. Many times it seems I had just stood up after a trial, only to be knocked down again by the next. It was God helping me to remember how it was that I got up, urging me to walk with Him, in His shadow, in His care."[2] Naaman's leprosy was terrible, and tragic, and uncomfortable, but so is the surgery that slices into our bodies and through our tissue walls to reach the cancer that is killing us. God wasn't just interested in healing Naaman's leprosy, He wanted to heal his soul. He wanted to remove the scales from Naaman's eyes so he could see and know who the real God was in the world.

Naaman would have been eternally grateful if the progression of leprosy simply stopped and got no worse. To have the leprosy removed from his skin would have been more than he could have hoped. But God did more. He gave him new skin, the skin of his boyhood, young, soft, and fresh. Why? Because our God is a God of love, and He delights in rewarding faith whenever He finds it. To coincide with Naaman's new heart and mind, God gave him new skin.

Naaman almost missed this as he was storming away with his pride and prejudices intact, and his leprosy firmly attached to both. It was a package deal. He couldn't lose the one without losing the other, and it is the same today. We would be naïve if we believed that Naaman came with any deep spiritual longings. He had one goal—to save his skin. God had a deeper purpose. He always does.

Last of all, Naaman learned:

---

[2]*A View from the Zoo,* Gary Richmond (Waco, Texas: Word Publishing), p. 45.

Listen to the painful truth

Does God work any differently today? No. Naaman was the poster boy for pride and prejudice, but God graciously sent trouble into his life that made him willing to change, to take a step of faith toward the one true God. How close did he come to making the wrong choice? How close are we?

It is so easy to see pride and prejudice in others and so difficult to identify it in ourselves. Yet if we ignore it in our own lives, our next decision could be tragic and defining. Naaman listened at the last possible moment—but he listened.

Are we prepared to make the right decision? Or will we let our pride and our prejudice drive us to make the wrong decision? If we're not careful we can spend too much of our lives listening only to those people who will tell us what we want to hear. Like David we must confess to God, "Behold, You desire truth in the innermost being" (Psalm 51:6). God wants us to be honest with ourselves about ourselves. Until we can become self-honest, we won't accept honesty from others about our true condition, and that could be disastrous.

Listen to people who may have wisdom that no one else will share with you. Often the people who love us most are the only ones willing to tell us the undiluted truth. Don't ignore them. They may be the ones God has sent as your final chance to make a right decision. Restrain your pride and prejudice. Don't allow them to keep you from taking that step of faith and trust in God.

Your greatest trial in life is sent not to destroy you but to heal you. The most defining moment in your life may be the moment you begin the process of removing imbedded attitudes of pride and prejudice. If you heed this advice, your greatest moment is still ahead of you.

DISCUSSION QUESTIONS

READ: 2 Kings 5:1–19

1. Think of something you do well that is a matter of pride to you. (It is not a sin to think realistically of such a thing; God gifts each of us in different areas).

2. Can you list any area in which you might be tempted to feel superior to others (education, income, intellect, looks, athletic ability)? Again, being tempted doesn't mean you have succumbed to the temptation.

3. Have you ever been guilty of pride or prejudice? Can you share one of those times?

4. We learned that Naaman had to humble himself to listen to people he ordinarily wouldn't. Make a list of at least three people or types of people you typically wouldn't seek out for advice. Why would you hesitate to listen to their advice? List both the good reasons and the bad.

5. Has God ever used someone to give you valuable advice that was not welcomed by you? Why was it so hard to listen to or accept their counsel? Do you have any regrets?

6. Why do you think God uses people we aren't in the habit of listening to, to share important truths with us?

7. Has there ever been a time in your life when an overwhelming desire to change made you willing to swallow your pride and seek help from someone you ordinarily wouldn't? What was the result?

8. Can you think of an issue in your own life so overwhelming that it is causing you to consider doing for God what you weren't willing to do before? Without necessarily mentioning the issue, share what you feel God may be trying to teach you through it.

Personal Reflection

We all have pride and prejudice, but we rarely address those problems until it is too late. God spoke to the prophet Balaam through the mouth of his donkey (Numbers 22:24–30). Whom has He been using to speak to you? For what special moment is He preparing you?

Follow-through

Ask God to bring to your attention any pride or prejudice you have been harboring, knowingly, or unknowingly. When He does (and He will) begin listing the names of people you need to humble yourself before and listen to. Continue to be open to others not yet on your list. Compare all advice against the Word of God.

THE STORY OF ACHAN

Then it came about on the seventh day that they rose early at the dawning of the day and marched around the city in the same manner seven times; only on that day they marched around the city seven times. And it came about at the seventh time, when the priests blew the trumpets, Joshua said to the people, "Shout! For the LORD has given you the city. And the city shall be under the ban, it and all that is in it belongs to the LORD; only Rahab the harlot and all who are with her in the house shall live, because she hid the messengers whom we sent. But as for you, only keep yourselves from the things under the ban, lest you covet them and take some of the things under the ban, so you would make the camp of Israel accursed and bring trouble on it. But all the silver and gold and articles of bronze and iron are holy to the LORD; they shall go into the treasury of the LORD."

Joshua 6:15–19

But the sons of Israel acted unfaithfully in regard to the things under the ban, for Achan, the son of Carmi, the son of Zabdi, the son of Zerah, from the tribe of Judah, took some of the things under the ban, therefore the anger of the LORD burned against the sons of Israel.

Now Joshua sent men from Jericho to Ai, which is near Beth-aven, east of Bethel, and said to them, "Go up and spy out the

land." So the men went up and spied out Ai. And they returned to Joshua and said to him, "Do not let all the people go up; only about two or three thousand men need go up to Ai; do not make all the people toil up there, for they are few." So about three thousand men from the people went up there, but they fled from the men of Ai. And the men of Ai struck down about thirty-six of their men, and pursued them from the gate as far as Shebarim, and struck them down on the descent, so the hearts of the people melted and became as water.

Then Joshua tore his clothes and fell to the earth on his face before the ark of the LORD until the evening, both he and the elders of Israel; and they put dust on their heads. And Joshua said, "Alas, O LORD God, why didst Thou ever bring this people over the Jordan, only to deliver us into the hand of the Amorites, to destroy us? If only we had been willing to dwell beyond the Jordan! O LORD, what can I say since Israel has turned their back before their enemies? For the Canaanites and all the inhabitants of the land will hear of it, and they will surround us and cut off our name from the earth. And what wilt Thou do for Thy great name?"

So the LORD said to Joshua, "Rise up! Why is it that you have fallen on your face? Israel has sinned, and they have also transgressed My covenant which I commanded them. And they have even taken some of the things under the ban and have both stolen and deceived. Moreover, they have also put them among their own things. Therefore the sons of Israel cannot stand before their enemies; they turn their backs before their enemies, for they have become accursed. I will not be with you anymore unless you destroy the things under the ban from your midst. Rise up! Consecrate the people and say, 'Consecrate yourselves for tomorrow, for thus the LORD, the God of Israel, has said,

"There are things under the ban in your midst, O Israel. You cannot stand before your enemies until you have removed the things under the ban from your midst." In the morning then you shall come near by your tribes. And it shall be that the tribe which the LORD takes by lot shall come near by families, and the family which the LORD takes shall come near by households, and the household which the LORD takes shall come near man by man. And it shall be that the one who is taken with the things under the ban shall be burned with fire, he and all that belongs to him, because he has transgressed the covenant of the LORD, and because he has committed a disgraceful thing in Israel.'"

So Joshua arose early in the morning and brought Israel near by tribes, and the tribe of Judah was taken. And he brought the family of Judah near, and he took the family of the Zerahites; and he brought the family of the Zerahites near man by man, and Zabdi was taken. And he brought his household near man by man; and Achan, son of Carmi, son of Zabdi, son of Zerah, from the tribe of Judah, was taken.

Then Joshua said to Achan, "My son, I implore you, give glory to the LORD, the God of Israel, and give praise to Him; and tell me now what you have done. Do not hide it from me." So Achan answered Joshua and said, "Truly, I have sinned against the LORD, the God of Israel, and this is what I did: when I saw among the spoil a beautiful mantle from Shinar and two hundred shekels of silver and a bar of gold fifty shekels in weight, then I coveted them and took them; and behold, they are concealed in the earth inside my tent with the silver underneath it."

Joshua 7:1–21

Chapter Four

A FATAL
ATTRACTION!

*Identifying the symptoms of
tragic decision-making*

There is a sport that a few daring souls have begun to embrace called BASE, or extreme jumping. Its name is derived from the acronym for buildings, antennas, spans, and earth. Instead of jumping out of a plane and parachuting, these folks jump off tall buildings, high antennas, bridges, and cliffs, tempting fate and danger for the thrill of it. Because of its inherent danger, it is banned in most places.

Jan Davis was one of five BASE jumpers prepared to challenge one such ban in Yosemite's National Forest. The group had climbed to the 3,200-foot peak of Yosemite's El Capitan. Their jump was going to be a public protest to demonstrate that the jumps could be made safely.

65

Davis was sixty years old and a veteran of countless jumps in the last sixteen years. She was the fourth of five jumpers, and used borrowed gear because she didn't want hers to be confiscated by rangers waiting to arrest her on the valley floor. As her friends and family watched from below, she jumped, but her chute never opened. She fell to her death.[1] The newspaper account of her death read, "Chutist dies in ironic tragedy."[1] BASE-jumping is inherently dangerous. That is part of its allure. It was, for Jan Davis, a fatal attraction.

Like Jan Davis, each one of us has our own fatal attraction. While we may not consider ours nearly so dangerous, our fatal attractions can ruin our reputation, marriage, career, friendships, and dreams. Perhaps there is no more vivid example in the Bible of this danger than Achan.

Achan's story is found in the sixth chapter of Joshua. Israel had crossed the Jordan River and marched around Jericho for seven days as God had commanded them. The story is familiar to us. Perhaps not quite as familiar are God's specific instructions. Before the people were commanded to shout, which would bring down the walls of Jericho, they were reminded:

"And the city shall be under the ban, it and all that is in it belongs to the LORD; only Rahab the harlot and all who are with her in the house shall live, because she hid the messengers whom we sent. But as for you, only keep yourselves from the things under the ban, lest you covet them and take some of the things under the ban, so you would make the camp of Israel accursed and bring trouble on it. But all the silver and gold and articles of bronze and iron are holy to the Lord; they shall go into the treasury of the LORD" (Joshua 6:16–19).

Achan was there. Achan heard the ban, but the temptation proved too great to him, and he broke it. Unfortunately for all of Israel, the divine consequence of Achan's sin was that God would no longer go

---

[1]*Orange County Register,* "Chutist dies in ironic tragedy," Saturday, October 23, 1999, by Kiley Russell, *The Associated Press.*

before them and lead them to victory. Unaware of what Achan had done, Israel attacked a small outpost called Ai. What should have been an easy victory turned into an inglorious defeat, and thirty-six men of Israel were killed. Ai remained defiant and unconquered. The rest of Joshua chapter seven relates the dramatic way that God exposed Achan's sin to Israel, and his resulting confession.

Seven symptoms of a fatal attraction

From Achan's example we can discern seven symptoms of a fatal attraction that may be evident in our own lives. If ignored, they could lead to a defining moment not unlike Achan's —terrible, shameful, and destructive. But if we can identify them, there is great hope that we can disarm the ticking time bomb before it explodes in our lives.

The most obvious symptom is:

A fatal attraction never lies dormant

A fatal attraction is nothing more than a secret sin or sinful attitude or activity that we have allowed to bloom. It is something we find ourselves drawn to that we know is dangerous and sinful, yet we have convinced ourselves that it's safe for us. Perhaps we've even cultivated this attraction in private.

How long had Achan struggled with this problem of greed? This was not a momentary character lapse for Achan, but the natural result of a fatal attraction he had nurtured. Unfortunately, it was an attraction needing only the right opportunity—a defining moment—to prove his undoing. Achan's fatal attraction was a glaring chink in his spiritual armor that he had ignored. His desire for wealth had hideously devolved into greed of the first order.

Achan's motivations are common to us all. James exposes the process of temptation in every human heart when he writes, "Let no one say when he is tempted, 'I am being tempted by God'; for God cannot be tempted by evil, and He Himself does not tempt anyone. But each one is tempted when he is carried away and enticed by his own lust. Then when lust has conceived, it gives birth to sin; and when sin is accomplished, it brings forth death" (James 1:13–15). How graphically this is revealed in Achan's defining moment!

But beyond James' words there is, in Achan's own confession, the clear downward spiral of temptation and sin.

"When *I saw* among the spoil a beautiful mantle from Shinar and two hundred shekels of silver and a bar of gold fifty shekels in weight, then *I coveted* them and *took them*; and behold, they are *concealed* in the earth inside my tent with the silver underneath it" (Joshua 7:21, italics added).

He saw, he coveted, he took, he concealed.

Before we leave this scene it is good to remember that thousands of Hebrew soldiers saw what Achan saw when they invaded Jericho, but their own greed had not degenerated to the level of Achan's.

There is an enlightening equation we can derive from Achan's life.

A Fatal Attraction + Opportunity = Shame, disgrace, and loss!
There is latent within all of us a fatal attraction. We may ignore it, assuring ourselves that we have it under control. We may fear it, terrified that it may one day be our undoing.

Often we mistake the lack of opportunity with self-control, but as Achan shows, in the mercy of God we may never have been exposed to the right opportunity. At some point, Satan will be given permission to tempt us again, and the opportunity will be presented.

Each of us has a sensitivity to different temptations. Some of us are extremely susceptible to financial temptations, others to sexual temptations, while others are vulnerable to temptations of fame or power. As you review the downward progression that led Achan to ruin, can you identify your own position? How close to danger are you?

I saw. I coveted. I took. I hid.

Achan's defining moment came when he first laid eyes on the treasure he discovered, because at that critical moment something happened that even he didn't understand. An unaddressed perverted passion had grown too strong for him to control. Did it surprise even him?

Feed it, and it will grow!

The movie *Little Shop of Horrors* is the story of a small alien flower that comes into the life of a young employee at a plant store. While the flower looks strange to him at first, he does his best to try to keep it alive. But despite his best efforts and all conventional care it continues to die. It is only when he accidentally cuts his finger and a drop of blood dribbles on the plant that it perks up. He is shocked to discover that it subsists on blood.

Each day the young man pricks his finger and feeds the ravenous plant, and each day the strange plant grows bigger and stronger, demanding more and more blood. It finally grows to fill the whole shop and even commits murder to fulfill its unquenchable desire.

This is an apt picture of what happens to unaddressed passions within us. They do not remain dormant; they will demand attention, and we must either deny them—sending them back into the shadows—or feed them, making them stronger still.

I saw. I coveted. I took. I hid. One unaddressed evil passion in our lives is all it takes. Remember, a fatal attraction never lies dormant. But secondly:

A fatal attraction deafens us to God's work and voice

A quick review of the book of Joshua reminds us that Achan had been part of two tremendous miracles of God within a short period of time. First, he had walked across the Jordan River on dry ground as the water was miraculously held back in a heap. Second, he had witnessed an amazing miracle when the walls of Jericho came down. Just before this miracle, Joshua had told everyone not to touch anything that was under the ban. Achan knew exactly what he was doing. He showed no concern that God was active in Israel and ignored the miracles performed right before his eyes.

Additionally, chapter five indicates that Achan must have been one of the men who had been circumcised. Circumcision was a sign of the Hebrews' covenant relationship with God. Had Achan forgotten the implications of this so soon? How can a man witness such miracles of God and then let his greed run amok? Didn't he believe God would see what he was doing?

Achan's story highlights the devastating effect of an unaddressed sinful passion. Our desire to listen to God's Word wanes. We lose our appreciation for His works. When we embrace a sinful passion and allow it to grow strong in our lives, one of its first debilitating attacks is on our spiritual focus. To reach any goal—even an evil one—takes concentration and focus. We work, think, and strategize to reach what we most want. When that happens, we lose sight of everything else. It is inevitable.

Achan's greed was all he focused on in the end. He had stopped listening to God and appreciating His mighty works because all his senses were trained on one thing—greed. An unaddressed passion will slowly but surely deaden us to God's work and Word in our life. We will begin to tune out God's voice because it will present an unwanted obstacle to our sin, and we don't want our sin challenged; we want it fulfilled.

This is why Paul warned the young pastor Timothy, "The love of money is a root of all sorts of evil, and some by longing for it have wandered away from the faith, and pierced themselves with many a pang" (1 Timothy 6:10). We can insert any number of passions in that verse and the result would be the same. The love of power, fame, and lust are also roots of all sorts of evil.

Beware of wandering

As Paul noted, most of us "wander" away from the faith. It is a slow defection rather than an abrupt departure. We don't just turn our backs on God one day; it takes time for a sinful desire to develop the level of intensity that will cause us to ignore the scriptural wisdom we've adhered to for years.

After years of counseling people who have been caught in various sins, I have noticed a clear pattern of behavior. A slow exchange of passions, developed over time, causes people to lose interest in God's work and voice. It often happens so slowly, and they feel so confident of their spiritual convictions, that they fail to address the danger properly. Over time, they become oblivious to the danger. And then, in what appears to be but a moment, they fall.

One evening I was watching a documentary on strange creatures. This episode dealt with a predatory fish that had the extraordinary ability to burrow into the ocean floor, becoming completely camouflaged. While this odd fish was too slow to catch the smaller fish on which its diet depended, God had given it a long worm-shaped appendage on the top of its head that could wiggle freely. When the fish lay on the ocean floor and wiggled that appendage, it looked just like a real worm dancing about. The unsuspecting prey would swim by, become tantalized by the worm-like appendage, and prepare to devour it. But in a split second, the predator rose up and swallowed the little fish.

Nature reminds us that this kind of thing happens every day. The Bible reminds us that it happens to people as well. Like the small fish being tantalized by the worm-like appendage, we become oblivious to the danger because we have stopped listening to God's warnings. But the danger doesn't end there. A third symptom is that:

A fatal attraction stimulates the growth of other sins within us

Listen to God's assessment of Achan's activity. "Israel has sinned, and they have also transgressed My covenant which I commanded them. And they have even taken some of the things under the ban and have both stolen and deceived. Moreover, they have also put them among their own things" (Joshua 7:11). How frequently do we traffic in one sin, and soon begin to "change lanes" to avoid detection. When we embrace one sin it becomes necessary to resort to another. Not only did Achan steal, but he had to deceive everyone into thinking he hadn't.

"Sins are like circles in the water when a stone is thrown into it; one produces another," wrote Phillip Henry. "When anger was in Cain's heart, murder was not far off."

How often when someone becomes involved in scandal, drugs, alcohol, or immoral activity does lying and deception enter the picture? Deception becomes necessary to hide the first sin already committed. When President Clinton was accused of immorality with Monica Lewinsky, what was his immediate reaction? He lied to try to cover up his sin. But before we throw too many stones, is he so different from the rest of us? Who among us has not lied to cover up another sin? Did not King David try to cover up his sin with Bathsheba? One fatal attraction stimulates the growth of other sins within us.

Did Achan exhibit any concern for the thirty-six men who died? Did he care for their families, or for his responsibility in this? The answer must be no, because the lot would take quite some time to fall to him, and he had ample time to come clean.

So why didn't he care? He didn't care because the seeds of self-centeredness and self-preservation had been cultivated in his life, to the exclusion of compassion and conscience.

The great aircraft carriers of World War II were vital war weapons. They were always escorted by other ships to protect them. In the same way our fatal attraction requires other sinful "escorts" to keep itself safe.

We must not deceive ourselves. One nurtured sin waters other seeds of sin, which have fallen into the fertile ground of our wavering faith and they will quickly bloom. The idea that we can isolate a particular sin in our lives and restrain it from spreading elsewhere is a myth. The weeds of sin will always spread. Fourthly:

A fatal attraction blinds us to encroaching danger

Achan's response to the lot is a fascinating study in human nature. Achan clearly understood how the lot worked, but at each draw of the lot, as it drew nearer and nearer him, he adamantly refused to confess. Achan never came forward, which leads me to believe he didn't think he was actually going to be caught. This shouldn't surprise us. He had already demonstrated that he was deaf to God's work and voice.

The Hebrews used the lot to determine God's will. The lot may have been stones marked with either black or white paint, or as others have suggested, they may have been pieces of marked pottery. Why the lot? Because "The lot is cast into the lap, but its every decision is from the LORD" (Proverbs 16:33).

There were mountains of evidence that God was carefully watching over Israel in every way, but Achan's sinful passion blinded him to it. It's conceivable that he simply didn't believe he would get caught. If he had an inkling he might, he was too greedy to risk losing his treasure unless he was forced to. Remember that he now had in his possession the thing he wanted most in life, the thing he had risked everything to get. Maybe he even hoped the lot would implicate someone else.

Don't sacrifice wisdom

A fatal attraction blinds us to encroaching danger. Achan obviously had the will to sin, he lacked only the opportunity. But it's doubtful he recognized his own weakness, for that would require wisdom. Achan had sacrificed wisdom on the altar of greed long before.

The Illinois Department of Natural Resources reports that more than 17,000 deer die each year after being struck by motorists. According to the state wildlife director, the peak season for road kills is in late fall. Why? The bucks are in rut in November. As he says, "They're concentrating almost exclusively on reproductive activities, and are a lot less wary than they normally would be." Those words are so instructive: "a lot less wary than they normally would be."

But we are not islands, and the activities we become involved in, for good or evil, start ripples that touch all those around us. Tragically, our defining moment will not affect only us, because:

A fatal attraction infects and destroys those nearest us

We sense a twinge of injustice when we see all Israel punished for one man's sin, but we must remember that they had all entered a covenant

with God. They had willingly agreed to be His people, to be faithful and obedient to Him. It was a unique arrangement. God looked at them as part of a unit. Each one's sin affected the whole. They had entered this agreement willingly and freely, and God had taken it seriously. When we read further that his family was killed with him, we are further prompted to shout, "No fair!" The law said, after all, "Fathers shall not be put to death for their sons, nor shall sons be put to death for their fathers; everyone shall be put to death for his own sin" (Deuteronomy 24:16). Since this was part of the law, which Joshua knew thoroughly, it seems that Achan's family was complicit in his scheme.

It would have been difficult for Achan to dig a hole in his tent, deposit several large objects, and then cover them up without his family knowing. Apparently they were part of the conspiracy to remain silent. Here we see another tragic outcome of refusing to address a fatal attraction —it infects those around us.

The values of parents are learned by their children. Achan's newfound wealth couldn't help but make life better for everyone involved, could it? Is it possible to believe that Achan's greed was not noticed by his family? His own covetous passions were being conveyed daily to his own children.

Severing the ties that bind

Before we dismiss the offense as petty theft, remember that as a result of Achan's sin, thirty-six daddies didn't come home. Thirty-six families lost sons, fathers, and husbands. An entire army was demoralized and in danger of being attacked by other armies in the area who would gain courage from Ai's victory over Israel. God's protection had been removed from them. An entire nation was now in great danger. Why? Because one man refused to address a sinful passion in his life. It destroyed not only his own life but his family and thirty-six others.

When we lose control of our lives, our friends and loved ones are often injured in the crash. Achan was not the last person to lose far more than gold when his life careened madly out of control.

But far more than just our own family and reputation are at stake, for we also know that:

A fatal attraction shames God and His people

God's assessment of the situation is clear and unequivocal: "He has committed a disgraceful thing in Israel" (Joshua 7:15). Not only was Israel disgraced by Achan's action, but God was shamed by it. Achan never even considered the shame his action would bring. Perhaps this is the most tragic of all the characteristics of Achan and all those who are in the grip of a fatal attraction—he didn't care. His sinful desire was far more important to him than God's reputation.

Years ago one of the large churches in our area was rocked by a public scandal. A former president of a large parachurch organization who was an elder in the church and a Sunday school teacher was accused of molesting young girls at his home. The disgrace was intense.

What is worse is that this same man had been accused of similar activity twenty years earlier and nothing had been done about it. His fatal attraction had remained buried until it finally bloomed and could no longer be hidden.

As we approach our own defining moments we need to ask ourselves an important question. Is there something in our life that, if not addressed and brought to light, could soon bring shame to our family, our church, and God? There may be an even more important question: does the thought that our life could shame God and His church bother us very much? If it doesn't, we may be further along in our fatal attraction than we think. But the seventh and most serious of all the symptoms is that:

A fatal attraction steals from God what belongs to Him

Achan never saw the seriousness of the sin he was harboring in his heart, but Joshua did. Remember God's instructions? "And the city shall be under the ban, it and all that is in it belongs to the Lord" (Joshua 6:17).

Now look again at Joshua 7:23: "And they took them from inside the tent and brought them to Joshua and to all the sons of Israel, and they poured them out before the Lord. Why did they pour Achan's treasures out before the Lord? Because they were not Achan's, or Israel's, or Joshua's—they were God's!

In search of satisfaction

Every one of us, regardless of whether we consider ourselves poor or rich, will want something we don't or can't have. The Bible reminds us that this is an essential part of our fallen nature. "Sheol and Abaddon are never satisfied, nor are the eyes of man ever satisfied" (Proverbs 27:20). We may want someone else's popularity, income, possessions, spouse, reputation, job, authority, girlfriend, or boyfriend. God, from His heavenly treasury, gives to each of us precious gifts of relationships, talents, family, position, and finances, but they are His. When we court any sinful passion within us, we are secretly conspiring to take more than God has allotted to us. To conspire to take sinfully what God has not given is to steal from Him.

Could a fatal attraction in your life be a plan to steal from God? It's difficult in our consumer-conscious, materialistic society, to believe that God may not want us to have what someone else has, but it's true. If we can accept this truth it can be one of the most freeing things we've ever learned, relieving us of the drive to accumulate and compare with everyone else. If we can't accept this truth, it may be the last warning we are given.

A secret sin, a fatal attraction, can be the determinative factor in a tragic defining-moment decision—unless we realize it and address it beforehand.

I saw. I coveted. I took. I hid.

A defining moment, tragically caught on divine film for eternity. Will we address our own fatal attraction in time? Achan let the process go too far. We can still stop it. We must, and the sooner the better. Let our legacy read:

I saw. I was tempted. I resisted. I escaped.

DISCUSSION QUESTIONS

Read Joshua 6:15–19; 7:1–21

1. Try to name some attractions we can have in life that could ultimately spell disaster for us. They can be physical, mental, spiritual, or emotional.

2. The downward spiral of a fatal attraction is found in the words: He saw, he coveted, he took, he concealed. Have you ever found yourself taking these steps with something you're attracted to, and at what point was the pressure greatest?

3. There are all kinds of attractions to tempt us. What kind do you feel yourself most vulnerable to, and why?

4. How has an unaddressed sinful passion in your past affected your desire to listen to and appreciate God's Word and works?

5. Read 1 Timothy 6:10. Why do you think Paul used the word "wandering" away from the faith in this passage? What can we learn about the allure of money, or any other attraction in the life of a Christian from this word? What is Satan trying to do in our hearts?

6. Ironically, it seems that the more we are attracted to a danger, the less wary we become and the less willing we are to listen to warnings. Why do you think this might be?

7. Can you think of a situation in which one individual's fatal attraction significantly affected other people?

Personal Reflection

Is there an attraction in your life that is growing so strong that, if given the right opportunity, you might indulge it? Ask yourself how this decision would affect your loved ones and the reputation of Jesus Christ. A fatal attraction is a ticking time bomb which must either be diffused, or it will eventually explode. You are either actively diffusing the bomb or waiting for the explosion. Which is it?

Follow-through

Confess to God your secret fatal attraction and your feelings of powerlessness to overcome it. Be honest. Ask Him to strengthen you to resist this temptation and to send His servants to you to help you overcome this before it gets too late. Actively seek out a pastor, or a wise and godly mentor or counselor, to help you diffuse your bomb before it explodes.

RUTH'S STORY

Now it came about in the days when the judges governed, that there was a famine in the land. And a certain man of Bethlehem in Judah went to sojourn in the land of Moab with his wife and his two sons. And the name of the man was Elimelech, and the name of his wife, Naomi; and the names of his two sons were Mahlon and Chilion, Ephrathites of Bethlehem in Judah.

Now they entered the land of Moab and remained there. Then Elimelech, Naomi's husband, died; and she was left with her two sons. And they took for themselves Moabite women as wives; the name of the one was Orpah and the name of the other Ruth. And they lived there about ten years. Then both Mahlon and Chilion also died; and the woman was bereft of her two children and her husband.

Then she arose with her daughters-in-law that she might return from the land of Moab, for she had heard in the land of Moab that the LORD had visited His people in giving them food. So she departed from the place where she was, and her two daughters-in-law with her; and they went on the way to return to the land of Judah.

And Naomi said to her two daughters-in-law, "Go, return each of you to her mother's house. May the LORD deal kindly with you as you have dealt with the dead and with me. May

the LORD grant that you may find rest, each in the house of her husband." Then she kissed them, and they lifted up their voices and wept. And they said to her, "No, but we will surely return with you to your people." But Naomi said, "Return, my daughters. Why should you go with me? Have I yet sons in my womb, that they may be your husbands? Return, my daughters! Go, for I am too old to have a husband. If I said I have hope, if I should even have a husband tonight and also bear sons, would you therefore wait until they were grown? Would you therefore refrain from marrying? No, my daughters; for it is harder for me than for you, for the hand of the LORD has gone forth against me." And they lifted up their voices and wept again; and Orpah kissed her mother-in-law, but Ruth clung to her.

Then she said, "Behold, your sister-in-law has gone back to her people and her gods; return after your sister-in-law." But Ruth said, "Do not urge me to leave you or turn back from following you; for where you go, I will go, and where you lodge, I will lodge. Your people shall be my people, and your God, my God. Where you die, I will die, and there I will be buried. Thus may the LORD do to me, and worse, if anything but death parts you and me." When she saw that she was determined to go with her, she said no more to her.

Ruth 1:1–18

Chapter Five

WHEN THE CHOICE MEANS NO RETURN

It was the afternoon of April 4, 1943, when the crew of the B-24 bomber, *Lady Be Good*, departed Soluch airstrip on the coast of Libya on their first combat mission. Their target was Naples, Italy. Shortly after takeoff, the bomber group encountered a sandstorm which affected their engines. The lead plane crashed into the ocean.

Unfortunately, the lead plane also served as the navigation aircraft for all the other bombers. They had the expert navigators; the rest of the aircraft followed them. The bomber group was now on its own.

For some reason, the *Lady Be Good* turned back thirty minutes prior to reaching the target. On their return flight, they took the wrong course. Realizing they were lost, they began to use their navigation equipment. But by now it was night. Unaware of a tailwind and sensing that they must be near the Libyan coast, they radioed for a reference point to guide them. However, unknown to them, they had already passed the coast and were now well over the desert. They had passed their reference points. This would be their defining-moment choice. Either believe the instruments—which were working perfectly—or follow their hunch.

They ignored their instruments and trusted their instincts. Hours later, they ran out of fuel and crash-landed 440 miles into the desert. Most of the crew survived the crash, but perished later, lost in the desert.[1]

The fork in the road

Each one of us will come face-to-face with choices like the one the crewmembers of the *Lady Be Good* encountered. We'll have to choose between two different directions, both competing for our attention. Our instincts will tell us one thing, but our faith will tell us another—and we will be forced to choose between the two. One is the old, the familiar, the comfortable; the other is the new, the frightening, the unknown. These are fork-in-the-road decisions, where choosing one means abandoning the other. When your moment comes, what will *you* need to make the right choice?

Defining-moment choices are not aberrations in the human drama but the very essence of it. It could be marriage, a career choice, or countless other decisions. Choosing one direction eliminates the possibility of going in the other. Many people in Scripture faced the same kind of decisions, but none highlights this dilemma quite so poignantly as Ruth.

The story of Ruth begins with a famine in Israel. An Israelite named Elimelech, and his wife, Naomi, decided to journey with their two sons to the nearby country of Moab, where the living was better and food more plentiful. While there, the two sons married Moabite women. Then tragically, first the husband and then Naomi's two sons died. She was left only with her daughters-in-law, both Moabites, Orpah and Ruth.

---

[1]"Lady Be Good" B-24 Bomber, Quartermaster Graves Registration Search and Recovery, http://www.qmfound.com/lady_be_good_b-24_bomber_recovery.htm

The two women loved Naomi dearly. When she told them she was returning to Israel, they both wanted to come with her. Naomi tried to dissuade them, explaining that their prospects for remarriage would be bleak in Israel.

The choice to return to their Moabite families and gods and culture was the defining moment for Orpah and Ruth. Finally, Orpah decided to return home, but Ruth refused.

Ruth's decision to accompany Naomi back to Israel—a foreign land to her, far from all that was familiar—was to become her defining moment.

Each of us will face just such a decision some day, if we haven't already. We have a tremendous advantage over Ruth, for the Bible reveals to us the principles that guided Ruth in this no-turning-back decision. How can we learn to make a good defining-moment decision when it means no turning back? First of all, we must determine to:

Look beneath the superficial

Remaining with Naomi was going to change not only Ruth's circle of acquaintances, it was to alter her whole world. It wasn't like moving out of the state, with the possibility of returning later. Ruth was leaving her native country for good.

That's why it is fascinating that Ruth decided to choose Jehovah, the God of Naomi. Don't misunderstand; Ruth made the right choice, but it was an extremely difficult one. Look at the situation from a strictly human perspective. Naomi and her husband left Israel because of a famine. Ruth might have inferred that God wasn't able to bless the Israelites as much as the Moabite god Chemosh had blessed the Moabites. When we consider that Naomi's husband and two sons had died, it seems that Ruth had little reason to change her beliefs.

For Ruth to choose the God of Naomi above her own god Chemosh, and to abandon the religion she had grown up with in the middle of fertile and beautiful Moab, she must have sensed something far more significant in Naomi's life. What had Ruth seen in Naomi and her sons?

What was so attractive about Naomi's faith that overruled all Ruth had seen with her eyes?

Many religions, cults, and ideologies seem to work well when all is going smoothly. But these false philosophies hold no answers when real trouble hits. Naomi had lost everything of value: her husband, her sons, and her security. When Job experienced a similar loss, his wife told him to curse God and die (Job 2:9–10). But like Job, Naomi refused to turn her back on God. Although her heart was broken and her life shattered, she clung tenaciously to her faith—even when she didn't understand why God allowed her to suffer.

Before Ruth made her life-changing decision, she must have witnessed in Naomi a depth of faith in God and a strength that were missing from her own life and the lives of those around her. She saw something that others had missed—possibly because she was looking for it.

Seeing what others miss

For nearly seventy years, a painting hung inconspicuously in a dark corridor of a Jesuit center in Pennsylvania. The artwork, entitled *The Raising of Lazarus,* was thought to be a reproduction. But when the painting was loaned to the Reading Public Museum, director Dr. Robert P. Metzger took notice. He convinced the priests to let art experts authenticate the work. It was determined to be an original by Jacopo Tintoretto!

As Dr. Metzger said, "It could easily be part of the collection of the Louvre or the Vatican." The painting was appraised at two million dollars.

Ironically, the rector of the Jesuit center, the Reverend J. A. Panuska, said that until recently "nobody really paid much attention to it. It was overlooked. We just sort of hung it."[2] How easy it can be to miss the truly valuable possessions in life if all we focus on are the external trappings.

When faced with a no-turning-back decision, each of us must look beyond the superficial. We must resist the temptation to opt for the

---

[2]Article: "Renaissance Treasure Found in Pennsylvania," *The Associated Press* 11/24/99, AOL.

most convenient decision and instead ask questions that deal with the deeper issues of life. What do I want my life to mean? What significant values will I be affirming? Which values will I be rejecting? For what do I want my life to be remembered? What will happen to my faith, my character, my values, and my relationship with God and others in this decision? Every significant decision in our lives reveals our core values. Will my decision honor God or shame Him?

Typically, the only questions we concern ourselves with are, Will I be better off financially, socially, vocationally, or emotionally? Will this decision increase my personal peace and affluence?

David Russell wrote, "The hardest thing to learn in life is which bridge to cross and which to burn." The answer is rarely the obvious one. Don't make your next no-turning-back decision without looking deeper than the superficial issues of money, status, convenience, and personal gratification.

But it's misleading to say there isn't a cost to making the right decisions. While digging beneath the surface will help us identify and affirm the values we want to drive our decision, there is more to consider.

We come to the second principle that guided Ruth in her defining moment:

Be willing to trade creature comforts for a higher purpose

"But Ruth said, 'Do not urge me to leave you or turn back from following you; for where you go, I will go, and where you lodge, I will lodge. Your people shall be my people, and your God, my God. Where you die, I will die, and there I will be buried. Thus may the Lord do to me, and worse, if anything but death parts you and me'" (Ruth 1:16–17).

These are two of the most famous and beautiful verses in all of Scripture. They contain an amazing confession of love and faith. Israel was not Ruth's country. It was not as fertile and productive as Moab. In Moab, Ruth had security and family. In Israel she would have an aging widow as her only relative. Where would she live? Israelites had little love for Moabites; wars and troubles between the two countries were common.

Naomi had been urging Ruth to return to her own family, friends, and community where she could almost certainly marry again and live a comfortable life—but Ruth responded by saying, in essence, "Don't ask me to do that. That stuff's not important to me anymore. My God is your God—there is no turning back for me anymore."

Before we etch these words onto a placard, let's put them in perspective. All this meant one thing to Ruth—no turning back! Her decision was final, no matter what the cost. Her old life was history. She no longer wanted to dwell in comfortable Moab; she desired to live forever in God's eternal kingdom. Her words were actually inviting poverty, loss, and isolation from all she had ever known. She knew nothing of Boaz, whom God would ultimately provide for her as a husband, or the marvelous ways God would bless her, making her the grandmother of King David. She looked directly down the barrel of a bleak future, and said, "Life as your friend and as a godly woman is more attractive to me than anything I'm giving up."

Ruth had to realize that during her lifetime she might never have what others did. But she must also have felt that what she was gaining eternally by joining herself to Jehovah was worth the temporal loss.

Did she make a bad choice? Be careful how you answer that. One day you will be faced with the same decision. When we live in a world of materialism—where money, popularity, and power are the reigning gods—and look at the successes others enjoy, how does it compare with what we see in a sacrificial life lived for God?

Are the most popular people in the world, the richest people in the world, the most powerful people in the world usually Christians? No! Then has God failed us? Is Christianity a bust? Is it still wise to serve and follow Him? We need to ask why so many people give up those gods to follow an itinerant, poor Galilean carpenter named Jesus.

The grueling taskmasters

All that the gods of materialism and ease can do is titillate and tantalize us. But they can't fulfill the deepest needs and answer the hardest questions life raises. According to a recent survey, the word most associated with the 1980s in America is the word *greed*. And what word did people use to describe the nineties? *Grueling*.[3] Materialism, popularity, and power are cruel taskmasters.

Ruth understood this. She was faced with the question Jesus would later ask, "For what does it profit a man to gain the whole world, and forfeit his soul? For what shall a man give in exchange for his soul?" (Mark 8:36–37).

Only Jehovah God could fulfill the deepest needs of Ruth's soul. Naomi's faith had taught her that there was purpose and meaning even in life's tragedies. An idol, no matter how charmed it might seem to be, couldn't offer real help. The God of Naomi was a personal God who desired a personal relationship with her. His will, character, and purposes had been revealed and they were holy and righteous. He was not a local god, but the only God, and the God of Moabites as well as Hebrews, if they would call on Him.

How much is enough?

In our accumulate-and-compare culture, it can be very tempting to worship at the altar of more. When success is defined by more money, newer cars, bigger houses, more power, and more fame, it's tough to make a decision that repudiates these idols. We know we will be branded for it.

Unfortunately, many of us have never asked ourselves the deeper questions. How much is enough? What will it take to satisfy me? What does that say about me? Is there ever a time when less truly is more? Is gratitude for what God has given me driving my decision? Or is it a burning desire for more?

Some of the most admirable people are those who live a simpler lifestyle than expected. They can afford to get bigger, better, and newer, but they don't. Some of these people are wealthy, others aren't. Wealth is an attitude revealed in priorities, not the size of a portfolio.

---

[3] *Orange County Register*, Business Monday: "Life and Work—FAST BREAK," Yankelovich Partners survey of work and life, 3/30/98.

Ruth consciously chose to forego the security she could have had in Moab for a day-by-day subsistence with Naomi in Israel. She wanted her life to be about more than "stuff" and the creature comforts. In following Naomi, she was really following God. She was refusing to allow the lust of the flesh, the lust of the eyes, and the boastful pride of life to make her decision for her. But don't think she wasn't tempted!

Have you asked yourself what you want your life to be about? Have you asked what God has called you to do for Him in the short time you have on earth? These are the kinds of questions that compel us to trade creature comforts for a higher calling.

When Jesus was tempted by Satan for forty days in the wilderness, the devil futilely tried to entice Him to turn the stones into bread. It seemed like such an obvious choice. Jesus was hungry. He had the power to provide His own food to alleviate the problem. Yet in His response, Jesus made it clear that creature comforts must never take precedence over obedience to God.

Our defining moment may come down to whether we will trade creature comforts for a more significant purpose in life. But there is one last principle to consider when making a decision in which there will be no turning back:

Choose the right models

Both Orpah and Ruth were faced with the same choice. But in chapter one, verses 10, 14, and 16, we can see the increasing determination Ruth showed in staying with Naomi. In verse ten, Orpah and Ruth both wanted to stay with their mother-in-law. Obviously they both loved her. Orpah decided to return to leave Naomi and her old life, but Ruth "clung to her" (v. 14). Then we read Ruth's great confession to Naomi, "Where you go, I will go" (v. 16).

Certainly Ruth had other models from which to choose. She must have had family members waiting for her, as well as community leaders and religious leaders. Naomi was a late arrival in her life. Yet, of all the role models Ruth had to choose from, she chose this Hebrew woman who believed in the God of the Hebrews, Jehovah.

Tell me who your role models are, and I can tell you what is most important to you. Whom you choose to emulate tells people what you value. We tend to use our models to help make our defining-moment decisions. We value what they value, which is why our defining-moment decisions reflect so deeply their influence on us.

Madonna or Mother Teresa

Often we select role models for their accomplishments. We admire their ability to accumulate wealth, or their athletic prowess, or their looks or courage. But Ruth reminds us to look deeper. Naomi seemingly had nothing going for her. She was poor, old, alone, and she wasn't overcoming her present difficulties—in fact, she was still despondent about them (Ruth 1:13). But what Ruth saw in Naomi was an unshakable faith in God even when He allowed painful experiences into her life.

What are the core values of your models?

Both Madonna and Mother Teresa achieved fame, but for radically different reasons. One indulges herself in every sensual pleasure she can. She schmoozes with the world's beautiful people, and enjoys wealth and popularity. The other denied herself these same sensual pleasures, not only living in poverty herself but traveling among the world's most destitute people. But consider this: if before Mother Teresa died you were told that one of these two had committed suicide—who would you guess it would be? Which one would be likely to deem her life so miserable as not to be worth continuing: Madonna or Mother Teresa? Yet whose values do most American girls choose to emulate?

Are you nearing a fork in the road, a point where you will be forced to make a no-turning-back decision? Here are three lessons to help you prepare for it:

• Be sure to look beneath the superficial. All that glitters is not gold.

- Be willing to trade creature comforts for a higher purpose. There is more to life than "more."
- Choose the right models in life, because there is a good chance you will turn out just like them.

One of the hardest things to learn is which bridge to burn, and which to cross. Choose wisely!

DISCUSSION QUESTIONS

Read Ruth 1:1–18

1. Are you facing a fork-in-the-road, no-turning-back decision right now? If you feel free to share this issue, please do.

2. We learn in Ruth that from a strictly human perspective some decisions make little human sense—yet are still God's leading. Take some time and list the pros and cons facing Ruth in her decision. Remember that she does not know what the future holds.

3. What might some of the intangible reasons have been for Ruth accompanying Naomi?

4. Ultimately, Ruth must have based her decision to accompany Naomi upon deeper life issues than simply material, social, and emotional security. If you had to make a "no-turning-back" decision, what would you base your decision on? What issues are most important to you?

5. What are some of the superficial issues that make no-turning-back decisions so difficult? Contrast those with your answers to the previous question.

6. What creature comforts would you be willing to forego in order to follow God's leading in your life?

7. Someone once said, "Tell me who you honor, and I'll tell you who you are." It is obvious that Ruth consciously chose Naomi out of all the people she knew to be her mentor and model in life. Who are your heroes and models in life, and what might that tell you about yourself?

8. Are you sensing a need to adopt different models in life, or different values to guide your decisions? Why, or why not?

Personal Reflection

Any values, or deeper purposes in our life, which are not drawn from God's word, will ultimately lead us to tragic defining moments. Begin searching God's Word, the Bible, to discover the deeper purposes for which God created you, and the values upon which you can safely prepare for a "no turning back" decision. Ask God to guide you in this endeavor.

Follow-through

Write down any major decisions you are facing. Then list the pros and cons of the decision, and then examine them. Ask yourself what deeper issues are at stake, and what you ultimately desire your life to be about. Consider how God would view the issue, and what He would consider important. And remember, as Ruth shows us, the obvious answer is not always the best.

ANANIAS AND SAPPHIRA

nd the congregation of those who believed were of one heart and soul; and not one of them claimed that anything belonging to him was his own; but all things were common property to them. And with great power the apostles were giving witness to the resurrection of the Lord Jesus, and abundant grace was upon them all. For there was not a needy person among them, for all who were owners of land or houses would sell them and bring the proceeds of the sales, and lay them at the apostles' feet; and they would be distributed to each, as any had need.

And Joseph, a Levite of Cyprian birth, who was also called Barnabas by the apostles (which translated means, Son of Encouragement), and who owned a tract of land, sold it and brought the money and laid it at the apostles' feet. But a certain man named Ananias, with his wife Sapphira, sold a piece of property, and kept back some of the price for himself, with his wife's full knowledge, and bringing a portion of it, he laid it at the apostles' feet. But Peter said, "Ananias, why has Satan filled your heart to lie to the Holy Spirit, and to keep back some of the price of the land? While it remained unsold, did it not remain your own? And after it was sold, was it not under your control? Why is it that you have conceived this deed in your heart? You have not lied to men, but to God." And as he heard these words, Ananias fell down and breathed his last; and great

fear came upon all who heard of it. And the young men arose and covered him up, and after carrying him out, they buried him.

Now there elapsed an interval of about three hours, and his wife came in, not knowing what had happened. And Peter responded to her, "Tell me whether you sold the land for such and such a price?" And she said, "Yes, that was the price." Then Peter said to her, "Why is it that you have agreed together to put the Spirit of the Lord to the test? Behold, the feet of those who have buried your husband are at the door, and they shall carry you out as well." And she fell immediately at his feet, and breathed her last; and the young men came in and found her dead, and they carried her out and buried her beside her husband. And great fear came upon the whole church, and upon all who heard of these things.

Acts 4:32–5:11

Chapter Six

AN IMAGE
TO DIE FOR

It was stunt motorcyclist Butch Laswell's big moment. In his very first movie appearance, he was to launch his motorcycle over the 38-foot-high pedestrian bridge next to the Oasis Hotel-Casino in Mesquite, Nevada—a record-breaking jump. Butch was concerned about ominous crosswinds that made his stunt much more dangerous. But a large crowd had gathered to witness the spectacular stunt, increasing the pressure to jump.

What to do? Laswell decided to risk his life rather than upset his fans. He raced his Honda CR500 up the ramp, accelerating to 85 mph, well above the 70 mph he had originally intended, perhaps to compensate for the wind. His goal was to clear the bridge by at least ten feet before coming down on the other side. However, it is estimated that Laswell soared to 58 feet above the bridge! He crashed to his death in front of movie cameras and thousands of spectators.[1]

What drove Butch Laswell to take that terrible chance? The desire to please other people, to convey to them that he was brave and daring. Obviously he'd had second thoughts about this stunt.

But there may be nothing we will risk more for than our public image. In Butch Laswell's case, he cultivated an image—a public perception—that cost him his life.

We want people to think of us in a particular light, even if that light doesn't reflect reality. We all desire to have a good image, and we spend quite a bit of time cultivating that image. The kind of house we buy, where we buy it, the kind of car we buy, the clothes we buy, the extracurricular activities we involve ourselves in all contribute to our "image." But the pursuit of that image can lead to dire consequences and a tragic defining moment.

Conflicting images

Image is so important that we will go to great lengths to create, nurture, and protect it. Many high-profile people hire image consultants. Companies, movie stars, and politicians spend billions each year on nothing more than image.

The average person is no exception. Consider the subject of clothing. When parents go shopping for clothes with their children, both parties are concerned with image. The clothes the kids wear will make a statement about them, and both the parents and youths know it.

But each party is trying to cultivate an entirely different image. The parents want to buy clothes that convey the image of "normal, healthy, respectable, and sane." The kids want to buy clothes that say—well, something significantly different.

---

[1] *Orange County Register*, Nation Briefly: "Stunt motorcyclist dies trying to please fans," 3/12/96, News, p. 4.

Why do young men wear pants so baggy that you could hide an entire Volkswagen in them? Then they belt them down around their knees so that they are forced to buy nothing but extra large T-shirts to cover areas of their anatomy that once were covered by pants. Is this more comfortable or practical? No, they are constantly trying to keep them up. Have you ever seen a kid try to run in such clothing? It's all about image. Everybody at school wears them that way, and they want to be an "individual"—just like everyone else! But are they so different from those of us who must have just the right house in just the right neighborhood with just the right car?

We may think that cultivating an image is a new idea, but it is, in fact, an age-old problem. Its source is not in the media or in advertising but in our fallen human nature. People have always been painfully concerned with what others think of them. The urge to create a better impression can be a more powerful enticement to deceive others than almost anything else.

Two people in the early church, a man and his wife, are striking examples of the danger of cultivating an image that does not reflect reality. This moment cemented them in time as surely as the lava from the eruption of Mount Vesuvius trapped those who tried to flee from its deadly reach. Forever they are remembered for their defining moment. Their names were Ananias and Sapphira.

When we approach the story of Ananias and Sapphira, we discover several examples of corrupt thinking that contributed to their disastrous defining-moment decision. They didn't simply make a last-minute blunder that had serious consequences; rather, they fell victim to a set of wrong ideas they had been harboring. Deceitful notions implanted in their hearts, when combined with their disregard for the Holy Spirit's conviction, pushed Ananias and Sapphira like mice through a maze to a deadly trap. As you examine this story, ask yourself if this dangerous mindset is finding refuge in your own heart.

The first evidence of corrupt thinking in the hearts of Ananias and Sapphira was:

They didn't believe that God would interrupt their sin

Acts 4:32–37 provides the background. Believers in the early church who owned land or houses would often sell them and bring the proceeds to the apostles. The purpose was that none of the believers should go without while others had plenty. A man named Barnabas, who would become famous as Paul's missionary partner, displayed one example of such giving.

The first verse of chapter five of Acts begins with the word "but." The recognition that Barnabas and the other generous members had gotten must have made a lasting impression on this couple. They were led less by a desire to help others than they were by the fame it would bring them among the church.

Ananias and Sapphira represent the people Jesus railed against. They use philanthropy as a stage upon which they can call attention to themselves. They coveted a reputation like Barnabas's.

Their sin consisted not so much in greed as in hypocrisy. They were pretending to donate the entire price of their land to the Lord's work, when in actuality they were keeping some of the cash for themselves. Evidently the couple didn't believe God would do anything about their sin.

We use make-up to cover blemishes. Certain clothes can make us look smaller, taller, or thinner. We live in houses and drive cars that we really can't afford to keep up our image. That's hypocrisy. It's a lie we're trying to foster, an image we're portraying that simply doesn't reflect reality. But since cultivating images is so prevalent, we can do so without thinking. We can get so used to fooling people that we believe we can fool God the same way. This is a spiritual cancer, and our loving God will surgically remove it if He has to.

Secrets will be revealed

There is a saying, "They'll carry that secret to their grave." The idea is that some things will never be known. But they will be—every single one. The Bible makes it clear that all the secrets we try to hide will be revealed. In Matthew 10:26 Jesus said, "There is nothing covered that will not be revealed, and hidden that will not be known." In Romans 2:16 Paul reminds us, "God will judge the secrets of men through Christ Jesus." Again, in 1 Corinthians 4:5, Paul said, "Therefore do not go on passing judgment before the time, but wait until the Lord comes who will both bring to light the things hidden in the darkness and disclose the motives of men's hearts; and then each man's praise will come to him from God."

What secrets will God reveal? Those things we tried to hide, those things we never confessed, those things we didn't want anyone to know. But it does not appear that God will expose any sins which have been openly and clearly exposed by us first. John tells us, "If we confess our sins, He is faithful and righteous to forgive us our sins and to cleanse us from all unrighteousness" (1 John 1:9). God knows each and every secret. With Ananias and Sapphira, most people saw a generous contribution, but God saw something different and revealed it to Peter.

In his book, *Men at Work*, author and political commentator George Will writes, "Baseball umpires are carved from granite and stuffed with microchips . . . . They are professional dispensers of pure justice. Once when Babe Pinelli called Babe Ruth out on strikes, Ruth made a populist argument. Ruth reasoned fallaciously (as populists do) from raw numbers to moral rightness: 'There's 40,000 people here who know that last one was a ball, tomato head.' Pinelli replied with the measured stateliness of John Marshall: 'Maybe so, but mine is the only opinion that counts.'"[2] No amount of poll-taking or public relations will disguise the truth from God.

In our defining moments we need to keep before us the abiding truth that God knows our hearts and searches them. He hates hypocrisy of any kind, and He will expose it. We may be lulled into complacency because our deception is not immediately exposed, but therein lies the great danger. We confuse God's mercy with inattention, or a lack of concern. This was one of the mistakes of Ananias and Sapphira.

---

[2]George Will, *Men at Work: The Craft of Baseball* (Macmillan Publishing Co., Inc., 1990).

Then the foolish couple compounded their problem with an unholy desire. Their thinking was corrupt in this way:

They craved a reputation they didn't deserve

Remember, Ananias and Sapphira had conspired to tell the lie. Since they had claimed they were devoting everything to God but really weren't, they might well have gained a reputation they didn't deserve. To deserve that reputation would have meant considerable personal sacrifice to God—a commendable act. But instead they tried to gain a good reputation at a discount. In the end they came up short. Trying to get something for nothing, they got far more than what they bargained for.

How many Christians have had tragic defining moments because they desperately wanted to possess a spiritual reputation they didn't deserve? Instead of being spiritual, they settled for sounding spiritual. Instead of being moral, they settled for appearing moral. Instead of being a true servant, they settled for looking like a servant. Instead of truly following Jesus, they settled for Christian bumper stickers and WWJD bracelets.

When we try to make ourselves look better than we are, we commit the sin of Ananias and Sapphira. When we pretend to be more spiritual than we are, we commit the sin of Ananias and Sapphira. When we distort information about ourselves, or events, or activities we have been involved in, we commit the sin of Ananias and Sapphira.

Their sin wasn't about money, it was about hypocrisy. It was about trying to portray a spiritual image that they and God knew didn't fit reality. God will not remain neutral in these moments. His goal in our lives is real, not ornamental, holiness. In 2 Corinthians 7:1 Paul says, "Therefore, having these promises, beloved, let us cleanse ourselves from all defilement of flesh and spirit, perfecting holiness in the fear of God." We must examine our own motivations and ask whether we are perfecting holiness, or merely polishing our "Christian" image.

Too good to be true

Brother Eagle, Sister Sky: A message from Chief Seattle, is a children's book that has sold hundreds of thousands of copies. In the book, Chief Seattle is quoted as saying those now famous words, "The earth is our mother," and "I have seen a thousand rotting buffaloes on the prairie, left by the white man who shot them from a passing train."

The only problem is that Chief Seattle never said those words. The chief lived in the Pacific Northwest. He never saw a buffalo. Those very quotable and now famous words were in fact written by a screenwriter named Ted Perry for *Home*, a 1972 film about ecology.

It seems that Perry wanted Native American testimony on environmental problems, so he made up some homilies and stuck them in Chief Seattle's mouth. Since then, this "gospel" has been widely quoted in books, on TV, and even from the pulpit.

Even Chief Seattle's only lone photograph has been doctored repeatedly. In the original, his eyes were closed. Subsequent photos were retouched so his eyes appeared to be open, and in later editions, his head was grafted on to the body of another man. The ironic part is that when Ted Perry tried to correct the impression he had made by setting the record straight, no one cared. Chief Seattle's image was now chiseled in stone, and no one wanted the truth.[3]

That's the problem with creating a false image—it gets harder to correct as time goes by. When Ananias and Sapphira's defining moment came, they simply did what they had become accustomed to doing. A defining moment is not a surprise, it is inevitable. It's not a momentary slip, it is a tragic habit finally exposed.

We must ask ourselves a hard question: Is our spiritual reputation deserved, or is it as fake as Chief Seattle's "speech"? If it is fake, the pretense won't last for long. God will expose it. But if we are honest,

---

[3]Article, "Just Too Good to Be True" by Malcolm Jones Jr., *Newsweek*, 5/4/92.

and we work to shatter any myths people might have developed about us, we can begin to change the outcome of our defining moment. Belief and desire will eventually harden into stone. This will lead to the third example of corrupt thinking that we see in Ananias and Sapphira:

They decided to let Satan into a corner of their lives

Those whom we allow to influence us will ultimately determine what we do. Remember Peter's statement: "Satan has filled your heart" (Acts 5:3). Through a wrong way of thinking that Ananias and Sapphira had never addressed, Satan had gained a foothold in their lives. There is no indication that Ananias and Sapphira were not true Christians. Christians can lie and cheat if they ignore the Holy Spirit and follow Satan's promptings and deceptions in their life.

In C. S. Lewis's classic book, *The Screwtape Letters*, he describes a correspondence between a demon and his young protégé, Wormwood, who is learning the ropes about how to afflict Christians. Lewis writes:

"Prosperity knits a man to the world. He feels that he is 'finding his place in it,' while really it is finding its place in him. His increasing reputation, his widening circle of acquaintances, his sense of importance, the growing pressure of absorbing and agreeable work, build up in him a sense of being really at home in earth, which is just what we want. You will notice that the young are generally less unwilling to die than the middle-aged and the old. The truth is that the Enemy, having oddly destined these mere animals to life in His own eternal world, has guarded them pretty effectively from the danger of feeling at home anywhere else."[4]

Satan is actively vying for the attention of Christians. Just because he can't possess you or keep you out of heaven doesn't mean he can't still influence you. Where is Satan most active in our lives? Hypocrisy! If he can turn us into hypocrites, no one will listen to our message about God! In reality, Ananias and Sapphira might have been respectable

---

[4]C. S. Lewis, *The Screwtape Letters*.

Christians in every area but one. But Satan needs entrance into only one part of a life to destroy it.

Give him an inch, he'll take a mile

The story is told of a villager who wanted to sell his house. Another man wanted to buy it, but because he was poor he couldn't afford the full price. After some bargaining, the owner agreed to sell the house for half the original price with one stipulation: he would retain ownership of one small nail protruding from just over the door. It seemed a trifle, so they agreed. After several years, the original owner wanted the house back, but the new owner was unwilling to sell it. So the first owner went out and found the carcass of a dead dog and hung it from the single nail he still owned. As the corpse rotted, the house became unlivable, and the family was forced to sell the house to the owner of the nail. The lesson is clear: if we leave the devil with one small peg in our life, he will return to hang his rotting garbage on it, making it unfit for Christ to use effectively.

Look around at the many prominent Christians who have fallen into sin. Does it appear that you need to immerse yourself in the occult before Satan can ruin your life and witness? No. Simply allow him one door, one area of your life, and tell him he can stay, and he'll wreak havoc. As someone once said, "The devil is easy to identify. He appears when you're terribly tired and makes a very reasonable request which you know you shouldn't grant." Your defining moment can be determined by one seemingly small area you've allowed Satan to gain access to. We see, then, another fatal flaw in Ananias and Sapphira's corrupt thinking:

They found evil fellowship in the practice of sin

It seems clear that the idea to lie originated with Ananias. Then he discussed it with his wife, and she eagerly agreed. He enjoyed "his wife's full knowledge" (Acts 5:2). Then "Peter said to her, 'Why is it that you have agreed together to put the Spirit of the Lord to the test?'" The couple had conspired to lie to the church and, even more seriously, to

the Holy Spirit. What might have happened had Ananias suggested this plan and Sapphira opposed it?

This practice of evil fellowship is ruining the reputation of the church of Jesus Christ. Christians develop confidence in sinning when they find others who will join them in it, especially people they respect. When a Christian becomes involved in questionable, immoral, or dishonest activity, their customary defense is "Well, so-and-so is doing it." "The pastor of that church did it." "I know an elder who did it." "That Christian celebrity did it." Yes, but are they acting like Christians when they are doing it? That is the more important question.

Too many Christians believe there is a fine line between godliness and sin, and our life consists of continually and perilously straddling a narrow fence. Nothing could be further from the truth. There is a huge chasm, a wide gulf, between godliness and sin. The godly person doesn't ask, "How close can I come to sin without actually getting involved?" The godly person asks, "How far can I stay away from even the appearance of evil?"

Picture what would have happened if Adam and Eve had taken this approach. Since their literal command was not to eat the forbidden fruit, perhaps they could have licked it. After all, technically that is not eating it. If they pounded on it with a big rock and made fruit juice, would it have been a sin to drink it? They wouldn't be eating it. That is the way carnal Christians, Christians who have not yet decided to seek holiness fully, approach their Christian life. They are constantly looking for loopholes. But the godly believer says, "I'm staying as far away from that tree as I can possibly get, I don't even want to be in the area." People do find evil fellowship in the practice of sin. They start to believe that if others are doing it, they can too, without any real consequences.

Is your defining moment going to be influenced by someone with even lower standards than yourself? If so, where do you think that will lead you? It doesn't matter what the school board, or the pastor, or the deacon, or anyone else is doing. What does God say? What does He want you to do?

The image gap

A spiritual reputation you truly deserve can be a great blessing, but should never be something you try to manipulate through deception or lies. If you discover you have a spiritual image you don't deserve—and part of that is a result of your own devices—it's not too late to change course.

In more than twenty years of ministry, I have never seen a Christian who exposed his or her own sin and was not received warmly if they did it in true repentance. It does not make us think less of the individual, it makes us think more of him. Transparency is refreshing, and it takes courage. Deception is discouraging and breeds resentment, heartache, and destruction.

Image is what others perceive us to be. Reality is what God knows us to be. The distance between these two is our image gap. The wider the gap, the greater the danger. The greater that gap becomes, the closer we are to reaching a tragic defining moment. Close the gap now, while there is still time. Your reputation depends on it.

DISCUSSION QUESTIONS

Read Acts 4:32–5:11

1. How do you think other people perceive you? What strengths and weaknesses might your close friends list if asked about you?

2. If you could imagine the "perfect you," how would you describe yourself? What would be your greatest strengths?

3. How accurately do others perceive and interpret your spiritual life? Why might someone's perception of you be different than your own?

4. On a scale of 1-10, ten being best, rate how you feel others would grade your spiritual health. Using the same scale—and a healthy dose of honesty—how do you believe God would rate you? If there is a discrepancy between the two, how do you account for it?

5. Why do you think it is so hard for us to be honest and transparent about our true spiritual condition with others?

6. In Acts 5:3, we read that Satan "filled" Ananias's heart. What does this mean? What do you think would have to happen in a Christian's

life for Satan to be able to fill and control them for a period of time as he did Ananias and Sapphira?

7. "Christians develop confidence in sinning if they can find others who will join them in it: people they respect." Have you ever been tempted to do something you knew was wrong because a Christian you admired did so? How did you respond?

8. "Image is what others perceive us to be. Reality is what God knows us to be." Would you be willing now, in a moment of transparency, to confess your image gap to the others in the group?

Personal Reflection

If we are honest, we will admit that we all have an image gap between what people think and what God knows. If we close that gap voluntarily God won't need to, and we will find freedom from trying to hide the truth. This isn't an excuse to sin freely, but the freedom to work openly on the real issues we are struggling with and enlist others in the process of healing.

Follow-through

Warning: This is only for the brave of heart! Write down your greatest spiritual weaknesses and temptations and then share them with two or three trusted Christian friends. Ask them to begin to pray for you that God might strengthen you, and that your spiritual image might be more closely aligned with reality. Read Psalm 51, written by David, for inspiration and encouragement.

THE STORY OF RAHAB

hen Joshua the son of Nun sent two men as spies secretly from Shittim, saying, "Go, view the land, especially Jericho." So they went and came into the house of a harlot whose name was Rahab, and lodged there.

And it was told the king of Jericho, saying, "Behold, men from the sons of Israel have come here tonight to search out the land." And the king of Jericho sent word to Rahab, saying, "Bring out the men who have come to you, who have entered your house, for they have come to search out all the land." But the woman had taken the two men and hidden them, and she said, "Yes, the men came to me, but I did not know where they were from. And it came about when it was time to shut the gate, at dark, that the men went out; I do not know where the men went. Pursue them quickly, for you will overtake them." But she had brought them up to the roof and hidden them in the stalks of flax which she had laid in order on the roof. So the men pursued them on the road to the Jordan to the fords; and as soon as those who were pursuing them had gone out, they shut the gate.

Now before they lay down, she came up to them on the roof, and said to the men, "I know that the LORD has given you the land, and that the terror of you has fallen on us, and that all the inhabitants of the land have melted away before you. For we have heard how the LORD dried up the water of the Red Sea before you when

you came out of Egypt, and what you did to the two kings of the Amorites who were beyond the Jordan, to Sihon and Og, whom you utterly destroyed. And when we heard it, our hearts melted and no courage remained in any man any longer because of you; for the LORD your God, He is God in heaven above and on earth beneath. Now therefore, please swear to me by the LORD, since I have dealt kindly with you, that you also will deal kindly with my father's household, and give me a pledge of truth, and spare my father and my mother and my brothers and my sisters, with all who belong to them, and deliver our lives from death." So the men said to her, "Our life for yours if you do not tell this business of ours; and it shall come about when the LORD gives us the land that we will deal kindly and faithfully with you."

Then she let them down by a rope through the window, for her house was on the city wall, so that she was living on the wall. And she said to them, "Go to the hill country, lest the pursuers happen upon you, and hide yourselves there for three days, until the pursuers return. Then afterward you may go on your way." And the men said to her, "We shall be free from this oath to you which you have made us swear, unless, when we come into the land, you tie this cord of scarlet thread in the window through which you let us down, and gather to yourself into the house your father and your mother and your brothers and all your father's household. And it shall come about that anyone who goes out of the doors of your house into the street, his blood shall be on his own head, and we shall be free; but anyone who is with you in the house, his blood shall be on our head if a hand is laid on him. But if you tell this business of ours, then we shall be free from the oath which you have made us swear." And she said, "According to your words, so be it." So she sent them away, and they departed; and she tied the scarlet cord in the window.

Joshua 2:1–21

Chapter Seven

HANGING BY A SCARLET THREAD

Sudden Decisions with Long-term Consequences

On a commuter flight from Portland, Maine, to Boston, pilot Henry Dempsey heard an unusual noise at the rear of the small aircraft. He turned the controls over to his copilot and went back to check it out. As he reached the tail section, the plane hit some turbulence, and Dempsey was tossed against the rear door. He quickly discovered the source of the mysterious noise. The rear door had not been latched properly, and it flew open. He was instantly sucked out of the jet.

The copilot immediately radioed the nearest airport, requesting permission to make an emergency landing. He reported the loss of the pilot, and asked that a helicopter search the area of the ocean they had been flying over. After the plane landed, they found Henry Dempsey—holding onto the outdoor ladder of the aircraft. Somehow he had caught the ladder, held on for ten minutes as the plane flew 200 mph at an altitude of 4,000 feet, and then, upon landing, kept his head from hitting the runway, which was a mere twelve inches away. It took airport personnel several minutes to pry Dempsey's fingers from the ladder.[1]

There are moments in which you must make a decision that will determine your future. You may be deciding on a move, or a career change, or any situation where the window of opportunity will stay open only briefly, then be shut forever. Your decision may leave you feeling like Henry Dempsey, hanging on by your fingers with all you've got. It's as if you are hanging by the proverbial thread.

Yet your decision will be influenced by a number of issues that can be studied beforehand, to help prepare for that moment. There is a biblical account of someone who experienced just such a moment. Her name was Rahab.

Rahab was faced with a momentous decision—one in which her life literally hung by a single scarlet cord. Like the threads woven together to make that cord, Rahab's moment of decision had several vital strands that comprised her successful defining-moment. The first strand is:

Her personal history

Rahab is one of Scripture's heroes of the faith (Hebrews 11:31). Unfortunately, she is best recalled for her sinful history, not for her wonderful acts of faith. Other heroes of the faith are remembered for their greatness. There is Moses the deliverer, David the giant-killer, Elijah, who slew the prophets of Baal. Then comes Rahab—the harlot. That label has stuck with her to this day.

Some well-meaning commentators have attempted to whitewash over her profession by calling her an innkeeper instead of a harlot. There are two

---

[1]*Leadership Magazine,* To Illustrate: "Holding On," as told by Greg Asimakoupoulos.

problems with this. First, ancient-Eastern innkeepers were never female. Second, there is a Hebrew word for innkeeper, and it is not the word used here. The Hebrew word used to describe Rahab's occupation is the word for *prostitute*. Rahab ran a small-scale Canaanite brothel out of her home.

There is no evidence that Rahab felt any shame at all over her vocation. From what we know of Canaanite culture and religion, she may have been a respected businesswoman or a religious prostitute. The Canaanites did not have the written law of God. They didn't know about the holiness of this God named Jehovah. They worshiped Baal and the Babylonian gods.

The Canaanite culture was horrible, with a detestable religion that required, among other grossly immoral practices, the sacrifice of the firstborn child to the gods. God had given them time and warning to repent, but they didn't. The children of Israel were to become God's instrument of judgment upon them, as other countries would later be to Israel when they disobeyed God.

On the wrong end of a promise

Rahab was a citizen of a land filled with people who customarily performed unspeakably evil acts. This was the way of Canaan. But as reports about the Hebrews trickled in to Jericho, she heard of the miraculous power of their God, Jehovah, the only true God. Rahab began to realize there was a difference between her gods and the God of these Israelites. He did not merely promise help, He delivered!

Rahab understood she was on the wrong end of that promise. This God was more powerful than her gods were. Her response to the spies shows us that they had been led by God to the one and only citizen of Jericho whose heart was ready to believe.

Who would have guessed that Rahab the harlot, of all those in Jericho, was the closest to faith? Her story teaches us that we can never judge a person's spiritual condition with a passing glance. Should that surprise us? Who most accepted and listened to Jesus when He came?

It wasn't the "righteous" religious crew. They rejected Christ! But those who listened most intently to Jesus were "publicans and sinners."

Our past often determines where we want to go in the future—and that helps us decide what we are willing to give up. Our experiences shape the values from which we will make our decisions. These experiences can completely change us, and prepare us for a dramatically different future.

A radical shift

Eldridge Cleaver is an amazing example of a dramatic spiritual turnaround. During the tumultuous sixties, Cleaver was the "minister of information" for the militant Black Panther party. He and his comrades advocated arson, robbery, rape, and murder as a way of balancing the scales of racial injustice.

Then, in 1968, Cleaver found himself in a shootout with Oakland police. His Black Panther colleague, Bobby Hutton, was killed. Cleaver was arrested, and he fled the country while his trial was pending.

For eight years, Cleaver traveled mostly in communist countries. As an avowed Marxist, he had expected his self-imposed exile to be an affirmation of all that was wrong with the democratic way of life. But after seeing the police brutality under Marxist regimes, he said, "It made me miss the Oakland P. D. It made me take a second look at what I was shooting my mouth off about." Cleaver took a closer look at his own history, which included two grandfathers who were Protestant preachers, and he decided to turn himself in.

Eldridge Cleaver spent fifteen years in prison for crimes that included attempted murder and possession of narcotics. During that time he returned to his Christian faith. But that faith was weak, and he lapsed into drug abuse. A brush with death cured his craving for drugs forever. Today he says, "We have got to get back to some of the oldest ideas in the world, and that is that God is love."[2]

---

[2]*Orange County Register*, Accent: "Radical Shift," by John Hughes, 4/23/98.

Of all those who we would be expecting to be preachers of the gospel, a man with a history like Eldridge Cleaver's would be among the last. But his past brought him to the place where he could hear God. When we start to seek God's wisdom, we are equipping ourselves to make wise decisions. But that choice is complicated when we consider a second strand that comprised Rahab's defining-moment decision:

The decision is irrevocable

Rahab had a choice. Her first option was the easy one. But it was a short-sighted view that told her, "Stay the course. Everything is going well. You have a comfortable life. If you turn in these two Hebrew spies, you could become a hero."

But what advantage is there, Rahab must have thought, *to be a comfortable hero in a doomed city?*

It is tempting to think to ourselves, *Perhaps my life doesn't count for much, and maybe I have never taken a stand for my faith, or for my God, but life is pretty comfortable. I don't want to do anything that might rock the boat. The key to life is just playing it safe.*

Every irrevocable defining moment tests our loyalties. In that sense, every single one of us is faced with Rahab's decision. To whom will we be loyal? We can be popular and comfortable in our Jericho, or we can throw in our lot with the new kingdom.

But Rahab couldn't choose both. Neither can we. Rahab determined that either the Hebrews were going down in defeat, or Jericho was. She had to make her choice. So do we.

This was not an easy decision for Rahab. Jericho was well-irrigated and beautiful, the garden spot of Canaan. To make her decision for God meant her world would never be the same. A Hebrew victory would mean she would lose her livelihood—in fact, her way of life would be considered a terrible sin! Her home would become a pile of rubble, and she would escape with only her family.

Faith moments

When John Newton, the one-time slave trader who authored the hymn *Amazing Grace*, accepted Christ, it cost him his livelihood. When William Murray, son of atheist Madelyn Murray O'Hare, accepted Christ, it cost him his relationship with his mother, his wife, and his oldest daughter. When Chuck Colson accepted Christ and then pleaded guilty in the Watergate affair instead of trying to lie and fight the charge, he lost his freedom. Defining moments are not trivial decisions, they forever alter our life. They are faith moments.

Why would Rahab do this? Where would she find the courage to make such a leap of faith in a God she did not know? The book of Hebrews gives us the answer: "All these died in faith, without receiving the promises, but having seen them and having welcomed them from a distance, and having confessed that they were strangers and exiles on the earth. For those who say such things make it clear that they are seeking a country of their own. And indeed if they had been thinking of that country from which they went out, they would have had opportunity to return. But as it is, they desire a better country, that is a heavenly one. Therefore God is not ashamed to be called their God; for He has prepared a city for them" (Hebrews 11:13–16).

Rahab was exchanging her old country for the heavenly one. She had caught a glimpse of God's power, and she knew that was what she wanted. In Hebrews 11:31 we read, "By faith Rahab the harlot did not perish along with those who were disobedient, after she had welcomed the spies in peace." By what? By moxie, self-confidence, and believing in yourself? No, by faith!

Defining moments can be irrevocable. They are also frequently fraught with danger. The next strand in the cord of a defining-moment decision that forever alters the future is:

The element of personal risk

Defining moments that honor God always involve personal risk. Either our reputation, relationships, or livelihood will be in jeopardy. For Rahab, everything was at stake. Had the king found the spies before they escaped, she was done for. If she had successfully helped the Hebrews and yet not put out the scarlet rope, she would also have perished. Finally, she trusted the Hebrews—complete strangers to her—to tell her the truth.

With all those unknown factors, how did she know what to do? Rahab chose to go with the God of the Hebrews because she had watched what God had done. She had heard about His great miracles on behalf of Israel. She knew she had to act. The help of God does not preclude human activity, it presupposes it. Rahab's life hung by that scarlet rope. It was something she had to do—not pray about, think about, or meditate on, but do! Defining moments mean taking action!

In your defining moments, God will require action to validate your faith. No matter what Rahab believed about God, no matter how convinced she was of the Hebrews' victory, no matter what her heart may have felt, if she hadn't hung out that scarlet rope, it would have all been for naught. James points out, "And in the same way was not Rahab the harlot also justified by works, when she received the messengers and sent them out by another way? For just as the body without the spirit is dead, so also faith without works is dead" (James 2:25–26).

Three military recruiters visited a high school to address the senior class. Each recruiter was allotted fifteen minutes to speak. The Army and Navy recruiters got long-winded and used up all the time. So when the Marine recruiter got up, he had only two minutes left. He walked to the microphone and stood absolutely silent for one full minute. Then he said, "I doubt whether there are two or three of you in this room who could even cut it in the Marine Corps. But I want to see those two or three immediately in the dining hall when we are dismissed." Then he turned smartly and sat down. There was a mob waiting for him in the dining hall.[3] This man knew how to appeal to someone's higher motivations, and that's what God calls us to do.

Satan always appeals to our lowest motivations. He reminds us of our personal convenience and safety. God appeals to our greatest motivations—courage and faith.

In your own defining moment, what are you willing to risk? The risk is not without hope. In fact, hope is the last strand we will consider in Rahab's defining-moment decision.

The hope of a better future

Everything Rahab knew God would do to her world, He did. Her home was gone, her livelihood lost, she and her family were strange Canaanites in the midst of the holy Hebrews. She and her family were saved, but saved to what? How would God treat her, a prostitute who had reached out to God for mercy?

Rahab and her family became Hebrews by faith after they were adopted into the Jewish community. How would the Hebrews accept this Canaanite harlot? When we come to God, He accepts us as we are, but He never leaves us that way. As Jericho had been buried in its own rubble, so Rahab's past was buried in the mercy of God. Rahab learned the law of God, a prerequisite to becoming a Jewish convert. Her faith and her love for Jehovah made her a new woman.

Then God brought along a man named Salmon, the son of Nashon, who saw in Rahab not a prostitute but a godly woman with an attractive faith. He married her. They had a son named Boaz, who gave them a grandson named Obed. Obed's mother was Ruth, who was also a Jewish convert, a former Moabitess. Obed was Jesse's father, and to Jesse was born David—King David of Israel. Through David's line would come the Messiah, our Savior Jesus Christ.

---

[3]*Leadership Magazine*, To Illustrate Plus, "Commitment," by W. Frank Harrington, p. 73, Spring.

Buried in Jericho—Raised in Christ

So did God allow His holy Son to have a prostitute in his ancestry? No. Remember, Rahab the harlot was buried in Jericho, and from those ashes, God created a godly woman. He's still doing that today. As Paul explained to the church at Corinth, "Or do you not know that the unrighteous shall not inherit the kingdom of God? Do not be deceived; neither fornicators, nor idolaters, nor adulterers, nor effeminate, nor homosexuals, nor thieves, nor the covetous, nor drunkards, nor revilers, nor swindlers, shall inherit the kingdom of God. And such were some of you; but you were washed, but you were sanctified, but you were justified in the name of the Lord Jesus Christ, and in the Spirit of our God" (1 Corinthians 6:9–11).

God never leaves those who come to Him in faith the way that He found them. He forgives them, cleanses them, and makes them new creatures in Christ. Hope fills their hearts and begins to affect their decisions, because they come to understand God's love for them. They can begin to interpret life's incongruities as the mysterious but wise moving of our heavenly Father. Fear of the future is replaced with hope in the Father.

The worst thing in life might not be making a wrong decision. The worst thing might be refusing to make a choice at all. And we will find that life crumbles in on us just like the walls of Jericho did. Remember, all of Jericho feared the Hebrews. All of them seemed to know they were doomed. Only Rahab acted, and only she escaped.

Is your life hanging by a thread? Faith is not something you wait for, like a letter to arrive in the mail, it is something you step out on, like a bridge over a raging river. God rescued and changed Rahab, and He has been rescuing and changing people ever since.

When you find yourself faced with a decision that has long-term consequences, consider the strands that made up Rahab's red cord:

- Her history
- The irrevocable nature of the decision
- The element of personal risk
- The hope of a better future.

All who trust in God's Son have been buried in Jericho and raised in Christ. As you face that irrevocable decision, remember, you have history on your side.

DISCUSSION QUESTIONS

Read Joshua 2:1–21

1. Have you ever experienced a time when you had to make a sudden decision with long-term consequences? How did you handle it? Would you have done anything different? Any regrets?

2. How do you think your past might positively affect a sudden decision you needed to make? How do you think your past might negatively affect such a decision?

3. Are you facing a decision now that will significantly change your life? These are faith moments. What spiritual issues or truths are you wrestling with in this decision?

4. What are the risks or fears you are facing in your decision?

5. What Scriptures come most to your mind and heart as you struggle with your decision? What do you feel God might be leading you to do?

6. Rahab's sinful past was buried in Jericho, and from those ashes He raised a godly woman, who would appear in the lineage of Christ.

How has God changed the person you used to be? What are the greatest changes He has made in you?

7. What were you most inspired by in the story of Rahab? Why?

Personal Reflections

Regardless of our background, each one of us is a Rahab before God, a sinner who needs grace. It is not what we once were that matters to God, but what He wants to make of us. Don't let your past discourage you. God is ready to forgive, cleanse, and transform you into the image of Christ. Always remember, we have been buried in Jericho, and raised in Christ.

Follow-through

Too many of us remain shackled by the sins of our past. The Old and New Testaments remind us that God wants to bury those sins and create a new life in Christ for us. It takes faith to trust God that our own personal Jericho is history to Him, but maybe, right now, that's what you need to do. Faith is an action, not an idea. We must stop visiting our Jerichos. Consider them buried and gone. Read and memorize Romans 8:1 and Colossians 3:1–3.

MOSES

Then the sons of Israel, the whole congregation, came to the wilderness of Zin in the first month; and the people stayed at Kadesh. Now Miriam died there and was buried there.

And there was no water for the congregation; and they assembled themselves against Moses and Aaron. The people thus contended with Moses and spoke, saying, "If only we had perished when our brothers perished before the LORD! Why then have you brought the Lord's assembly into this wilderness, for us and our beasts to die here? And why have you made us come up from Egypt, to bring us in to this wretched place? It is not a place of grain or figs or vines or pomegranates, nor is there water to drink."

Then Moses and Aaron came in from the presence of the assembly to the doorway of the tent of meeting, and fell on their faces. Then the glory of the LORD appeared to them; and the LORD spoke to Moses, saying, "Take the rod; and you and your brother Aaron assemble the congregation and speak to the rock before their eyes, that it may yield its water. You shall thus bring forth water for them out of the rock and let the congregation and their beasts drink."

So Moses took the rod from before the LORD, just as He had commanded him; and Moses and Aaron gathered the assembly

before the rock. And he said to them, "Listen now, you rebels; shall we bring forth water for you out of this rock?"

Then Moses lifted up his hand and struck the rock twice with his rod; and water came forth abundantly, and the congregation and their beasts drank. But the LORD said to Moses and Aaron, "Because you have not believed Me, to treat Me as holy in the sight of the sons of Israel, therefore you shall not bring this assembly into the land which I have given them."

Numbers 20:1–12

Chapter Eight

THE SLIPPERY ROCKS
OF SUCCESS

For Brian Smith, the pool created by a historic dam at Santiago Oaks Regional Park in Southern California was a magnet. He and his friends frequented it for the thrill of leaping off the cliffs that shelter the murky water twenty feet below and provide natural diving platforms. This was not the first time he had jumped these cliffs with his friends. They had done it often.

Posted signs prohibited swimming and wading, yet many people ignored the warnings. Some even jumped in the sight of the park rangers who told them to quit. But for Brian, the jump was even more tempting. As his mother, Cheri Smith, said, "If there was a mountain to climb, he would climb it."

At about 3:30 p.m., the boys were preparing to leave. But Brian wanted just one more dive. This time, to increase the thrill, he added a flip. It would be his last. Witnesses told rangers that Brian landed belly first in the water but didn't come up. His friends dove in after him and pulled him out, but it was too late. Brian died the next morning.[1]

It was not that one dive that doomed Brian, but rather a false sense of security. He had jumped so often without injury that he believed he would never get hurt. The warnings only applied to others. He and his friends were the exception. Brian was playing Russian roulette with his life. If you play a deadly game long enough, you will lose.

Lured by danger

Last year we went on a family-camping trip to Yosemite National Park with our church. We hiked around Hetch Hetchy Reservoir and discovered a place where smooth flat-rock surfaces and water running downhill combined to create a natural water slide. Some kids slid down on their backsides, others used air mattresses. All were having the time of their lives.

But there was one patch, blackened by continual water runoff, that was dangerously slick. As long as the kids were sitting down they were safe, but to stand up on that patch was asking for a knot on the head. The best solution was to avoid the area entirely, yet it drew the young people like flies to honey.

There are slippery spots in each of our lives, places where the wrong decision spells complete disaster. If we become accustomed to success in ministry or in the workplace we can be lulled into a false sense of security. We begin to believe we have the Midas touch, that we are the exception to the rule. The feeling that we are safely insulated from life's tragedies entices us to take moral and spiritual risks.

Can someone who really loves God and truly seeks to serve Him find himself slipping on his own success? The story of Moses at the waters of Meribah not only tells us that they can, but shows us the steps that lead to the fall. Success will put us on the path to these danger spots, but we

---

[1] *Orange County Register*, Metro: "Flip dive fatal for man," by Vik Jolly, 6/20/96.

can safely sidestep them if we plan ahead. Recognizing the slippery steps will prepare us to walk safely around them.

Moses was a magnificent man of God whose faith and godliness were eminently displayed. But in one critical moment, at the waters of Meribah, he made a decision that was to haunt him and deny him one of his most cherished desires. Ironically, a person can make a good decisions for a lifetime and yet one day make a foolish one that will define him in a tragic way.

The greater our responsibility, the greater the consequences for our mistakes. The miraculous water God promised and delivered through Moses was the very water that would spell disaster for him. His fall was painful, and the consequences sad.

Slippery surfaces

Our greatest stumbles can come when success seems to flow like a river through our lives. They are heady moments, but the flowing waters of success can create a slippery surface. And because success is also a high-altitude experience, the fall from such heights is even more devastating.

Can someone who really loves God and truly serves Him still slip on his own success? Yes, and it is more common than we realize. The story of Moses gives us four valuable insights to guard us in our own defining moments. How can we know we are on one of life's slippery surfaces? We find ourselves on one of these steps when:

We draw attention to ourselves rather than to God

The Hebrews were nearing the end of the wilderness wanderings that were God's punishment for their lack of faith. Once again, their sheer numbers had depleted the local water reserves. As was their unfortunate custom, they began to blame Moses and Aaron for all their problems.

It seems difficult at first glance to determine what Moses did that was so wrong. Moses served as the covenant mediator between God and the Israelites. Under God's covenant, or contract, with the Israelites, Moses

interceded before God on behalf of the people. Since the people were in need of water, Moses and Aaron went into the tent of meeting and sought the Lord. God assured them He would provide for them and told them exactly how. What was the big problem?

In verse four the Israelites asked Moses, "Why then have you brought the Lord's assembly into this wilderness, for us and our beasts to die here?" To whom were the people talking? They were talking to Moses, not to God. Verse five says, "Why have you made us come up from Egypt, to bring us in to this wretched place? It is not a place of grain or figs or vines or pomegranates, nor is there water to drink."

The Israelites put the spotlight on Moses, not on God. Unfortunately, Moses began to respond in kind. He understandably grew tired of their complaining and whining, but he began to take upon himself more authority and responsibility than belonged to him.

In verse 10 we read, "Moses and Aaron gathered the assembly before the rock. And he said to them, 'Listen now, you rebels; shall we bring forth water for you out of this rock?'" Moses was at the end of his patience with Israel. He called them rebels, which is exactly what they were. But in his anger he implied that he and Aaron were going to provide the water. By his angry words and rash actions, Moses directed attention not to God but to himself and Aaron. He diluted God's glory in this miraculous moment, and he knew better.

In showcasing his own feelings, Moses failed to set God apart as holy and the only One deserving glory. This was to be God's moment. When God intervenes in a miraculous way, He is parting the thin veil that separates the physical world from the spiritual world to give us a closer look at Himself. Moses, in effect, had jumped in front of that magnificent scene and said, "Hey, look at me, I'm really mad!"

It seems to us a small matter, but the act was witnessed by hundreds of thousands of people. Moses was supposed to be representing the holiness and righteousness of God to the Israelites, showing them how God would provide for them. It was a tremendous responsibility.

When we have been given a great responsibility, it is easy to get caught up in the spotlight that comes with it and forget the only One who is worthy of that spotlight.

We have a New Testament parallel to this situation. Paul related to the Corinthian church the great revelation that had been given to him by God and the resulting problems that accompanied it. Paul wrote, "Because of the surpassing greatness of the revelations, for this reason, to keep me from exalting myself, there was given me a thorn in the flesh, a messenger of Satan to buffet me—to keep me from exalting myself! Concerning this I entreated the Lord three times that it might depart from me. And He has said to me, 'My grace is sufficient for you, for power is perfected in weakness'" (2 Corinthians 12:7–9).

Why was Paul given his thorn in the flesh? We don't need to guess. Paul knew—it was to keep him from exalting himself. God's answer to Paul was, "My grace is sufficient for you."

Moses' sin, and ours, consists of drawing attention to ourselves rather than to God. God gives us abilities—mental, physical, spiritual—for a purpose. They are the tools He wants us to use in glorifying Him. We must determine not to allow our God-given abilities to glorify ourselves instead.

Do you have a God-given ability or gift that brings attention to yourself? There is nothing wrong with that—God has given you that gift. However, He gave you these things to act as reflectors of His glory, to direct all praise back to Him. As we bask in the warm glow of our success, it can be easy to forget why God turned that spotlight on in the first place.

A second way we know we are on a slippery step is when:

We take credit for the accomplishments of God

As the children of Israel began to give Moses and Aaron credit for what had happened to them, both good and bad, Moses neglected to correct them. He should have reminded the people that God alone was responsible for both their deliverance and their present dilemma.

When you are surrounded by people willing to give you earthly credit for heavenly activity, it becomes easy to go with the flow. You may realize you weren't responsible for these acts, but God used you to accomplish them, and that can make you feel important. It is heady stuff to be used to perform great things—in Moses' case, even miraculous things.

The more we find ourselves in the spotlight, the greater and more insidious are the temptations. Someone who would never think of lying or stealing, or being involved in sexual immorality or financial corruption—the more obvious sins—often falls prey to pride that tempts him continually in the form of sincere compliments. All a person needs to acquire "Balloonius Headius," as a friend of mine calls it, is too much attention.

Those of us in leadership are especially vulnerable to stumbling. We can begin to take just a tiny bit of the credit for God's work through us. When we start taking bows for God's work, we slip on the wet rocks of success. Moses may have started to believe his own press clippings. He wouldn't be the last.

We also know that life's steps are slick when:

We intentionally ignore God's clear directives

Look at verse 8 and take note of God's clear directions to Moses. "'Take the rod; and you and your brother Aaron assemble the congregation and speak to the rock before their eyes, that it may yield its water. You shall thus bring forth water for them out of the rock and let the congregation and their beasts drink.'" The command was to speak to the rock. But look at what Moses did. "Moses lifted up his hand and *struck the rock* twice with his rod; and water came forth abundantly, and the congregation and their beasts drank" (v. 11, emphasis added).

Moses didn't simply forget the instructions. God makes it clear he disobeyed. He went beyond what he had been told to do. God said, "You have not . . . [treated] Me as holy in the sight of the sons of Israel" (v. 12). Because Moses had always treated God as holy in the sight of Israel, God had given him more and more personal honor. But now, at the peak of Moses' popularity, he played the part of the angry leader and detracted from God's presence and glory.

The striking of the rock is widely interpreted as Moses' anger at the children of Israel. But his personal feelings and actions were now obscuring their view of who they were to be focused on—God, their provider, their sustainer, and their protector.

We can be faithful in so many things for so long, and God can give us greater and greater honor. Then one day we come to a clear directive from God and veer off the trail—ever so slightly, to our own minds— and that decision results in discipline from God. Why? Because of the principle that Jesus taught us: "And from everyone who has been given much shall much be required; and to whom they entrusted much, of him they will ask all the more" (Luke 12:48). The more we receive, the greater our responsibility from whom we received it.

When I was a teenager, I had a very visible and vocal faith in Christ. Mike was a guy who sat directly across from me in one of my classes. He was likeable, but he was a party animal. I was nice to him, but we never did anything together. One day Mike surprised me by inviting me to his house for a pool party, though he knew I was a Christian. Concerned that this would be a situation where questionable moral and even illegal activity might occur, I begged off. He said he understood.

Later that morning I was walking through the school hallway with a friend, and I was telling him how I wouldn't be caught dead at Mike's party. My friend kept elbowing me and whispering to me to shut up, but I wasn't paying any attention and kept talking. Finally, he pulled me aside and said, "Didn't you see Mike? He was right behind you, and he heard every word you said!"

I don't think I had ever done something so stupid. I heard later that Mike said to a friend, "If that's what a Christian is, I don't want to have any part of it."

God's reputation was at stake here. The hardest thing I ever did in my life was go to his house on the day of the party and apologize to him

for the stupid thing I said. He accepted my apology graciously, and I learned a valuable lesson.

To whom much is given, much is required. The greater our visibility, the greater our responsibility. When we ignore one of God's directives, the negative fallout will be much greater on us. What God will not require of someone else, He will require of you. Ignoring this principle is a good way to find yourself on the bad end of a defining moment, one that brings tragedy instead of joy.

Finally, we know our way is slippery when:

We feed an attitude of indispensability

After all God had used Moses to do, after all the incredible miracles He had used Moses to perform, Moses began to entertain some small sense of indispensability to God's program. Listen to the tone in Moses' words to the assembly of Israel. "Moses and Aaron gathered the assembly before the rock. And he said to them, 'Listen now, you rebels; shall we bring forth water for you out of this rock?'"

Moses is implying, "Listen, I've saved your bacon so many times before; do I have to do it one more time?" And it was true. Moses had interceded for Israel on several occasions when God was thoroughly disgusted with them. But each time Moses had been only the instrument; God was the Savior. Moses knew this deep-down, but he was developing a sense of personal pride rather than an attitude of grace.

I have had to learn the hard way that no one is indispensable. Wherever God raises up a Moses, He always has a Joshua in the background. Always. The results of Moses' poor decision are found in Deuteronomy 3:26–27. "The Lord was angry with me on your account, and would not listen to me; and the Lord said to me, 'Enough! Speak to Me no more of this matter. Go up to the top of Pisgah and lift up your eyes to the west and north and south and east, and see it with your eyes, for you shall not cross over this Jordan.'"

Ouch! The Hebrew grammar suggests Moses kept asking God for permission, pleading, so that God finally said "No!" in a loud and firm voice to settle the issue. Like the popular slogan, God had to ask Moses what part of "no" he didn't understand. One commentator writes, "The fact that even the greatest of God's servants cannot simply ask God for whatever they like and get it bothered people in the Old Testament times and continues to today. The fact that even they must sometimes leave this life without seeing the full fruit of their labors is also a problem. It was true with Moses and with Paul. But it is true to life. People share the incompleteness, which belongs to the human condition."[2]

It's a common temptation among those whom God greatly uses to be so excited about what God has done that they forget that He could have done the same thing through someone else. He chose us to highlight His glory, not our own abilities and gifts. We begin to feel no one else could do our job, at least not as well.

Playing for the Master

There is a story about Poland's famous concert pianist and prime minister, Ignace Paderewski. A mother took her young son to a concert by the master, to encourage his progress at piano. They took their seats up front, and while she started talking to a friend, the little boy wandered away and spied the big piano on stage. When the spotlights came on, the audience grew quiet. On stage was the little boy at the piano bench, playing "Twinkle, Twinkle, Little Star." Before his mother could do anything, Paderewski rushed on stage, came up behind the little boy, and whispered, "Don't quit; keep playing." Then he reached down with his left hand and began filling in a bass part, and with his right began a running obligato. Together they held the crowd mesmerized.

That's the picture of even the most gifted among us. We're playing "Twinkle, Twinkle, Little Star;" God is the Master filling in everything

---

[2] *Broadman Bible Commentary,* Volume 2, p. 199.

else. We're not indispensable to God's program; we're objects of His love and grace. He uses us so that we will enjoy the blessing, not because He has no other means to accomplish the job. As someone has said, "If you want to realize your own importance, put your hand into a bucket of water, take it out, and look at the hole."

Moses never entered the Promised Land—Joshua did. Moses learned he was not indispensable.

But there is a beautiful ending to the story. Although Moses could not enter the Promised Land, God graciously let him survey the entire territory. A number of commentators suggest that for Moses to have been able to see all that is described would have required a miraculous gift of vision. What grace and mercy! A momentary lapse that brought serious consequences was still only temporary. Moses viewed the Promised Land, and then God took him to his real home (Deuteronomy 34:1–7).

If we learn nothing else we must acknowledge that all earthly talents, gifts, honors, dreams, and ambitions must one day be given up. Our "Promised Land" will be realized in God's kingdom, not here and now.

How are you looking at the success God has given you? How are you treating the gifts and blessings He's brought into your life? The most difficult tightwire to balance on is success. It is a slippery platform, and our feet are unsure. When we try to stand to take a bow, we fall. The only safe position with success is on our knees.

Success is not to be feared or shunned. But like the beautiful rose, it most not be grasped carelessly, for it has sharp thorns. Take this to heart. Your next defining moment may depend on it.

DISCUSSION QUESTIONS

Read Numbers 20:1–12

1. As you look back upon your life, what do you think people would consider your greatest earthly success?

2. What do you consider to be your greatest earthly success?

3. How have you handled your success? If you had it to do over, what would you change about your reaction to it?

4. What is the greatest single challenge that success can present to us? Why?

5. Define "success" from a biblical perspective. In other words, how do you think God defines it?

6. In moments of personal spiritual success what can you do to help keep a healthy perspective?

7. How could spiritual success foster an attitude that we are indispensable to God? How could sincere compliments do the same thing?

8. Recount some success in your life, and evaluate in what way God was responsible for it. What might His purpose be in your success?

9. Is success a spiritual opportunity to glorify God, or a spiritual test? Discuss.

Personal Reflection

The greatest danger in spiritual success is that we can feel the moment of success is our defining moment. Yet, from God's perspective, the defining moment is how our character and heart handle the kudos and honors we receive. God created us to sincerely reflect all glory back to Him, not bask in it.

Follow-through

Determine today that God has a greater purpose for any success He brings into your life than personal glory. Success is not only an opportunity; it is a test. Ask God to change your heart regarding your personal success. Begin to change the way you view any and all worldly and spiritual success you experience, and actively look for what God might want to be doing through you, not simply to you, in your success.

THE STORY OF SHADRACH, MESHACH, AND ABED-NEGO

Then Nebuchadnezzar in rage and anger gave orders to bring Shadrach, Meshach and Abed-nego; then these men were brought before the king. Nebuchadnezzar responded and said to them, "Is it true, Shadrach, Meshach and Abed-nego, that you do not serve my gods or worship the golden image that I have set up? Now if you are ready, at the moment you hear the sound of the horn, flute, lyre, trigon, psaltery, and bagpipe, and all kinds of music, to fall down and worship the image that I have made, very well. But if you will not worship, you will immediately be cast into the midst of a furnace of blazing fire; and what god is there who can deliver you out of my hands?" Shadrach, Meshach and Abed-nego answered and said to the king, "O Nebuchadnezzar, we do not need to give you an answer concerning this matter. If it be so, our God whom we serve is able to deliver us from the furnace of blazing fire; and He will deliver us out of your hand, O king. "But even if He does not, let it be known to you, O king, that we are not going to serve your gods or worship the golden image that you have set up."

Then Nebuchadnezzar was filled with wrath, and his facial expression was altered toward Shadrach, Meshach and Abed-

nego. He answered by giving orders to heat the furnace seven times more than it was usually heated. And he commanded certain valiant warriors who were in his army to tie up Shadrach, Meshach and Abed-nego, in order to cast them into the furnace of blazing fire. Then these men were tied up in their trousers, their coats, their caps and their other clothes, and were cast into the midst of the furnace of blazing fire. For this reason, because the king's command was urgent and the furnace had been made extremely hot, the flame of the fire slew those men who carried up Shadrach, Meshach and Abed-nego. But these three men, Shadrach, Meshach and Abed-nego, fell into the midst of the furnace of blazing fire still tied up.

Then Nebuchadnezzar the king was astounded and stood up in haste; he responded and said to his high officials, "Was it not three men we cast bound into the midst of the fire?" They answered and said to the king, "Certainly, O king." He answered and said, "Look! I see four men loosed and walking about in the midst of the fire without harm, and the appearance of the fourth is like a son of the gods!" Then Nebuchadnezzar came near to the door of the furnace of blazing fire; he responded and said, "Shadrach, Meshach and Abed-nego, come out, you servants of the Most High God, and come here!" Then Shadrach, Meshach and Abed-nego came out of the midst of the fire. And the satraps, the prefects, the governors and the king's high officials gathered around and saw in regard to these men that the fire had no effect on the bodies of these men nor was the hair of their head singed, nor were their trousers damaged, nor had the smell of fire even come upon them.

Nebuchadnezzar responded and said, "Blessed be the God of Shadrach, Meshach and Abed-nego, who has sent His angel and delivered His servants who put their trust in Him, violating the king's command, and yielded up their bodies so as not to serve or worship any god except their own God. Therefore, I make a decree that any people, nation or tongue that speaks anything offensive against the God of Shadrach, Meshach and Abed-nego shall be torn limb from limb and their houses reduced to a rubbish heap, inasmuch as there is no other god who is able to deliver in this way." Then the king caused Shadrach, Meshach and Abed-nego to prosper in the province of Babylon.

Daniel 3:13–30

Chapter Nine

DEFINING-MOMENT FRIENDSHIPS

A missionary friend in Indonesia e-mailed me detailing the persecution the school and the believers were facing. Riots were breaking out, the political situation was inflamed, churches were burning with believers still inside them. Muslim radicals were behind most of the violence, aimed at the typical scapegoats: ethnic Chinese living in Indonesia—and Christians.

The violence began to get much closer to them. My friend wrote, "On January 21, an unknown group came at night and tore down the walls of a new dormitory that was just in its beginning stages of building. This site is a couple blocks from the main campus. Since that date there have been several times in which a mob came to SETIA [the Bible Institute] at night and threatened to burn the school down, banging the front gate, etc. In the meanwhile, classes have begun. The staff and the students are not going to leave and are willing to die there if necessary. They have gone to prayer more diligently than ever. They comfort themselves in singing a lot of praise songs to God."

Some of the momentous decisions we must make as Christians are not merely personal, they are collective. We must make certain defining-moment decisions with others. This circle may include Christian friends, family, fellow church-members, or brothers and sisters in Christ across the nation.

An incredibly powerful dynamic occurs when Christians stand together. We feed off each other's strengths and faith. An act of courage that might seem impossible on our own is made easier when we are with others of like mind and faith. One of the greatest benefits available to us is our close Christian friendships. They can be the determining factor to us to make the right decision.

Three brave young Jewish exiles provide the background for our focus on friendship. Their names are Shadrach, Meshach, and Abednego. They were faithful Hebrews, carried into captivity in Babylon by Nebuchadnezzar's armies. Because they showed great promise, they were trained to serve in the Babylonian government where they received prominent positions.

Then one day the pagan Nebuchadnezzar christened a new idol he had set up for himself, a huge golden image. All the officials of the province were ordered to attend the ceremony. At the appropriate signal, they were to bow down and worship the image.

To the Hebrews, this was idolatry and forbidden by God. Defying the king's command, Shadrach, Meshach, and Abed-nego refused to bow. Their conspicuous refusal gave their enemies the opportunity to tell the king. Infuriated, Nebuchadnezzar gave them one more chance to bow to the image.

Through what happened next to these three men, we can see the strength of common convictions, translated into three practical advantages. Advantage number one is that:

With others you can face danger with new courage

Some fears are unique to us as individuals, and we must, of necessity, face them alone. But there are common fears that confront other Christians as well. Opposition to our faith is common to all believers— not merely personal.

One fear I have is evangelism, and I know I am not alone in this. I recall the time I signed up for an evangelism training class in our church. I knew I needed to confront my fear of sharing my faith. One week I went with my instructor and another fellow trainee on a "cold call." These visits were my greatest fear. I did not enjoy showing up at the home of someone who was not expecting us. But my instructor was an experienced evangelist, and off we went.

When we arrived at the door and announced who we were and why we were there, I was terribly nervous. To my surprise, we were invited in. In the next hour-and-a-half we learned that this young man and woman who were living together had been attending Bible studies with a cult. Only recently had they prayed and asked God to show them what the truth really was. We became the answer to their prayer. They both accepted Christ, got married, and began to serve Him faithfully.

I could never have been part of that divine appointment without the other two believers with me. Their presence gave me greater faith. Jesus affirmed this truth by sending out His apostles in twos and threes, never alone.

Shadrach, Meshach, and Abed-nego had learned the strength of standing together. Look again at the punishment hanging over their heads. "But whoever does not fall down and worship shall immediately be cast into the midst of a furnace of blazing fire" (Daniel 3:6). And look at what it would mean to them. "There are certain Jews whom you have appointed over the administration of the province of Babylon, namely Shadrach, Meshach and Abed-nego. These men, O king, have disregarded you; they do not serve your gods or worship the golden image which you have set up" (Daniel 3:12).

It's difficult for those of us who enjoy religious freedom to appreciate the possibility of suffering, or even dying, for our faith. We feel persecuted if someone merely calls us names, such as "religious extremists," or "homophobes," or "Jesus Freaks," or "fanatics." But that is not true persecution.

Nothing to fear but fear itself

These three men were facing more than public humiliation and ridicule for refusing to bow to Nebuchadnezzar's idol. They were staring at certain death. And as if that bleak prospect weren't intimidating enough, they were to be burned alive.

President Franklin Delano Roosevelt lost the use of his legs to polio. His greatest fear was of being in a house fire, for he knew he would not be able to escape it. But it was FDR who said with such eloquence during World War II, "We have nothing to fear but fear itself." He knew what he was talking about.

Even the bravest among us have to deal with fear. Napoleon, himself a courageous conqueror, referred to Marshall Ney as the bravest man he had ever known. Yet Marshall Ney's knees trembled so badly one morning before a battle that he had difficulty mounting his horse. When he was finally in the saddle he shouted in disgust, "Shake away, knees! You would shake worse than that if you knew where I am going to take you!"

Shadrach, Meshach, and Abed-nego had much to lose. They had prominent positions administering in the province of Babylon in the presence of Nebuchadnezzar. It is likely they had known for quite some time about the great image. Such a large endeavor would have been hard to keep secret. These three friends had ample time to think, talk, and pray about what they should do, and then decide as a group their course of action.

They eventually chose the most dangerous course—one that would permit no turning back. They decided that when the time came to bow down to the image, they would remain standing and trust themselves to God's care. But they must have decided it together.

The Bible teaches that strong godly fellowship brings courage. Solomon writes, "Two are better than one because they have a good return for their labor. For if either of them falls, the one will lift up his companion. But woe to the one who falls when there is not another to lift him up. Furthermore, if two lie down together they keep warm, but how can one be warm alone? And if one can overpower him who is alone, two can resist him. A cord of three strands is not quickly torn apart" (Ecclesiastes 4:9–12).

Fighting fear with fellowship

Shadrach, Meshach, and Abed-nego all had fears, but they also had great faith. Their combined faith reminded each other of God's power and love for them, and helped grow a resilient, collective courage.

We may hesitate to take a step of faith alone. Yet we will take that courageous step when others are with us. Have you ever stood before a scary amusement park ride and heard one timid person say to another, "I'll go if you will." Consider the logic of that. The ride will be no less dangerous if you ride with that friend or not. But a fear shared is a fear lessened.

I took part in a pro-life walk-a-thon to raise money for a crisis pregnancy center. Some of us carried signs that were respectful, but clear about our position. Some people drove by and gave us dirty looks, unfriendly honks, or unmistakable hand gestures. But it was much easier to take because they were mad at us, not at me personally. I respected the lives and opinions of those I was walking with much more than those who disagreed with me, and that gave me courage. As someone has said, "Courage is fear that has said its prayers."

An important part of your defining moment as a family, as a church, as a group, will be the people closest to you. Those whom you surround yourself with will have a significant influence on what you do. They will either encourage you, or discourage you, from taking great steps of faith. But the strength of common convictions also provides for a second advantage:

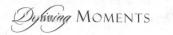

You will stand your ground with greater conviction

Taking a step of faith can be frightening. But an even greater challenge is standing your ground as the opposition intensifies. The biblical account says, "Our God whom we serve is able to deliver us from the furnace of blazing fire; and He will deliver us out of your hand, O king" (Daniel 3:17).

Notice those words, "whom we serve"? The three friends were not simply talking about the God they believed in, but the God whom they served. Many claim to believe, but few actually serve. The faith of Shadrach, Meshach, and Abed-nego was not a once-a-week activity. Their stand was completely consistent with the life of faith they lived out every day. At a young age, along with Daniel, they had refused to eat the king's choice food, a stand that could have cost them their lives (Daniel 1:1–16). Now they were taking an even greater stand—a literal stand. They chose to remain standing while everyone else bowed down.

In their defining moment, they made themselves conspicuous and vulnerable. Yet it must have been a tremendous encouragement for Shadrach, Meshach, and Abed-nego to look around and see each other standing up to be counted for God!

There is nobility and integrity in their refusal to bow. How easily they could have rationalized appeasing the king's anger. They might have said, "We'll bow our knees, but not our hearts." No, Shadrach, Meshach, and Abed-nego knew that people would see their timid actions and draw only one conclusion. There are times when we aren't able to explain our position, we have time only to act—and we must act immediately and decisively!

Or the three friends could have reasoned, "If we bow today, we'll live to serve God another day!" The lie we sell ourselves in situations like this is that if we compromise on this one issue, we'll be of more service to God in the end.

These attractive rationalizations can easily creep into our lives. The last thing Satan wants us to do is stand our ground and test the faithfulness of God. Did Satan try to whisper attractive compromises into these three men's ears? Undoubtedly. They must have been tempted to find some other solution to the problem, some graceful way to bow out of the corner their faith had backed them into. But they remained committed to one course of action, not only individually, but collectively. Their hearts were knit together by a common commitment. They were sons of Abraham and would worship only one God—no matter the cost.

That's what the strength of a common conviction will do for you. You will be enabled to hold your ground against the strong tide of popular opinion and the waves of pressure that accompany it.

The third practical advantage of common convictions is that:

Your faith can be taken to a higher level

At no time did any of these three men say, "Whoa, stop, I was just kidding! I've changed my mind. I plead temporary insanity!" When Nebuchadnezzar increased their torment by heating the furnace seven times hotter, they watched quietly. It must have taken some time to increase the intensity of the fire—time for them to reconsider, time to think about what they were going to lose, what they were leaving behind, time to dwell on the excruciating pain and suffering that awaited them.

As they were being carried to a furnace so hot it killed the men carrying them, what do you think they were doing? My guess is they were praying! There was nothing left to do. They were going to meet their Maker one way or another, they simply didn't know which way. The faith of Shadrach, Meshach, and Abed-Nego had been taken to the highest possible level. They were willing to be martyrs.

But they never felt the heat. The only things that burned up were the ropes used to bind them. The three friends didn't even break a sweat! In that furnace, the place that threatened to be their grave, they met the Son of God and had their faith validated as few ever have. Even Nebuchadnezzar praised their faith, because he realized they were completely and irrevocably committed to the one true God.

Bernard of Clairvaux wrote, "Only by desertion can we be defeated. With Christ and for Christ victory is certain. We can lose the victory by flight but not by death. Happy are you if you die in battle, for after death you will be crowned. But woe to you if by forsaking the battle you forfeit at once both the victory and the crown."

Coffee, tea, or He?

A pastoral associate gave me an article from *Time* magazine called, "Will it be coffee, tea or He?" The article was subtitled, "Religion was once a conviction. Now it is a taste." The author, Charles Krauthammer, writes from the perspective of a non-religious Jew, who was amused when going in for an outpatient test at a hospital. The woman who admitted him to the hospital asked the usual questions: name, insurance company, ailment. But then she inquired, "What is your religious preference?"

He writes, "The only reason hospital folk bother to ask about religion at all is prudence, not theological curiosity. In case they accidentally kill you or you otherwise expire on their watch, they want to be sure they send up the right clergy to usher you to the next level, as it were. We're not talking belief here, we're talking liability protection."

This led him to speak about religious intolerance. Quoting G. K. Chesterton, he writes, "Tolerance is the virtue of people who do not believe in anything." He argued, "Every manner of political argument is ruled legitimate in our democratic discourse. But invoke the Bible as grounding for your politics, and the First Amendment police will charge you with breaching the sacred wall separating church and state." Finally, he quotes Yale law professor, Stephen Carter, who calls this activity, "the culture of disbelief." This, Carter says, is "the oppressive assumption that no one of any learning or sophistication could possibly be a religious believer—and [includes] the social penalties meted out to those who nonetheless are. One is allowed to have any view on abortion so long as it derives from ethical or practical or sociological or medical considerations. But should someone stand up and oppose abortion for reasons of faith, he is accused of trying to impose his religious beliefs on others. Call on Timothy Leary, or Chairman Mao, fine. Call on St. Paul, and all hell breaks loose."

In conclusion he writes, "At a time when religion is a preference and piety a form of eccentricity suggesting fanaticism, Chesterton needs revision: tolerance is not just the virtue of people who do not believe in anything; tolerance extends only to people who don't believe in anything. Believe in something, and beware . . . you'll make yourself suspect should you dare enter the naked public square."[1]

Such is the age in which we live. These are our furnaces. We do not need to fear them. We must not let the good news of Jesus Christ be silenced. Let our world stoke the fires, let them make it seven times hotter. It's good for us. It goads us to take our faith to that next level. Let us stand ready to meet that moment. But how do we prepare for it? Will you be ready for your moment, if it comes at work this week, at home, in your community, in your nation?

The strength of a common conviction among believers will take each of us to higher levels of faith and practice than we could ever go alone. The Bible says, "As iron sharpens iron, so one man sharpens another" (Proverbs 27:17).

The strength of a common conviction enables us to face danger with more courage. It empowers us to stand our ground with greater conviction. It prompts us to take our faith to a higher level. But all this brings some hard questions we must ask.

The hard questions

Who are your Shadrach, Meshach, and Abed-nego? Who will stand with you? Our defining-moment friends are not heroes from afar but people close to us. These three were close friends who were held together not

---

[1] *Time,* essay by Charles Krauthammer, 6/15/98.

by personality traits or common weaknesses, like so many of our friend-ships, but by a common conviction about their faith.

Are your closest relationships encouraging or discouraging your Christian convictions? If your answer is discouraging, you are being prepared for your defining moment, but you will not be proud of the result. We must add to our circle of friends strong growing Christians whose convictions we admire, people who will respond to a defining moment with courage and faith.

Are you rushing toward an imminent defining moment in life and faith woefully unprepared? There is a solution. Find those whose faith and life you respect, and begin spending more time with them and less with the discouragers. Seek out the encouragers! Don't abandon your non-Christian friends or your weaker Christian friends, but don't allow them to drag you down either. Be the one to raise, not lower, the stan-dard among your peers.

If you do this, your faith will be strengthened, your Christian convic-tions will be reaffirmed, and you will be made ready for any defining moment God might bring into your life. It is not the fire of the fur-naces that is important, but the fire of our faith, lighted by Christ and stoked by Christian brothers and sisters standing with us in our defining moments.

DISCUSSION QUESTIONS

Read Daniel 3:13–30

1. List some of the significant decisions that we need to make as a group, rather than as individuals.

2. Have you ever faced a difficult decision that was made easier by the presence and support of other like-minded Christians? What was it? How was it easier to make the decision with others?

3. What are some spiritual activities which are made easier with the encouragement and presence of other believers?

4. My closest Christian friends would certainly strengthen me in a tough spiritual decision or action (circle a response below and then explain your answer).
   - I don't think so.
   - I'm not sure, I hope so.
   - I'm pretty sure they would.
   - Yes, absolutely.

5. Can certain Christian friends or acquaintances we have actually weaken our spiritual resolve? How? Why?

6. Name your Shadrach, Meshach, and Abed-nego. (List at least three.)

7. What positive effect do these friends have on your Christian faith and walk?

8. How have you been used to strengthen a fellow Christian's faith or walk?

9. List the ways you have grown most significantly as a result of your defining-moment friendships.

Personal Reflection

God provides all the spiritual resources we need to make great defining-moment decisions, but sometimes we don't make use of them. Strong Christian friends are not optional, they are standard equipment in the body of Christ. Remember, you not only need defining friendships, you need to be a defining friend to someone else.

Follow-through

Write down the names of those Christians closest to you whom you count on for strength and encouragement. Call or write them and tell them why you consider them to be your defining-moment friends. Explain how you count on them, and that you want them to count on you. Ask them how you can pray for them or help them in some issue or struggle. If you don't have such friendships, seek out Christians you admire and ask them if they'd be willing to be prayer partners with you. Be faithful to pray for others, and check back with them regularly.

THE WIDOW'S MITE

And He sat down opposite the treasury, and began observing how the multitude were putting money into the treasury; and many rich people were putting in large sums. And a poor widow came and put in two small copper coins, which amount to a cent. And calling His disciples to Him, He said to them, "Truly I say to you, this poor widow put in more than all the contributors to the treasury; for they all put in out of their surplus, but she, out of her poverty, put in all she owned, all she had to live on."

Mark 12:41–44

And He looked up and saw the rich putting their gifts into the treasury. And He saw a certain poor widow putting in two small copper coins. And He said, "Truly I say to you, this poor widow put in more than all of them; for they all out of their surplus put into the offering; but she out of her poverty put in all that she had to live on."

Luke 21:1–4

Chapter Ten

MONEY AND THE DEFINING VIRTUES

Not long ago, billionaire Ted Turner made a remarkable announcement. At a press conference it was revealed that Mr. Turner was donating one billion dollars to the United Nations. One billion dollars! This was news! All over the world the message was sent by newspaper, radio, and television. Ted Turner was displaying his generosity in a very public way. Accolades began to stream in—what a great guy! What a class act! What a wonderful moment! Surely history was being made. Who ever gave so much before?

Few things reveal more about us than the way we spend our money. Jesus told us, "Do not lay up for yourselves treasures upon earth, where moth and rust destroy, and where thieves break in and steal. But lay up for yourselves treasures in heaven, where neither moth nor rust destroys, and where thieves do not break in or steal; for where your treasure is, there will your heart be also" (Matthew 6:19–21). That last line is telling. "Where your treasure is, there will your heart be also."

In light of Ted Turner's obvious act of charity, it is instructive that Jesus drew attention to a gift from someone at the opposite end of the financial spectrum. This individual was making not the world's largest contribution, but perhaps the world's smallest contribution—at least in monetary value. She was not a billionaire; she was destitute. She did nothing to call attention to her gift. There was no press conference. In fact, she was completely unaware of the significance of her own defining moment. No one paid any attention to her tiny contribution—no one except for Jesus.

While this widow was giving her minuscule donation to the Lord in the temple, Jesus was watching. He found her act so incredible that He called to His disciples and pointed it out to them. From that moment to this, the story of the widow's mite has become world-famous and has received far more "press" than Ted Turner's gift can ever hope to get.

Some defining moments involve money, but aren't really about money. These defining moments will simply highlight the absence or presence of four essential financial virtues that are characteristic of those who are faithful to God. If we are cultivating these four defining virtues in our lives, our financial defining moments will be flattering. If we are not, they will be shameful.

J. Oswald Sanders said, "Money is one of the acid tests of character and a surprising amount of space is given to it in Scripture. Whether a man is rich or poor, observe his reaction to his possessions and you have a revealing index to his character."[1]

If we want our financial defining moments to be memorable, we need to discover these four virtues and incorporate them into our own lives. As we look at these four virtues so wonderfully modeled by the widow,

---

[1] *A Spiritual Clinic,* by J. Oswald Sanders, as quoted in *Illustrations Unlimited,* p. 374, #28.

we need to ask ourselves whether they are evident in our own financial decisions. The first virtue is:

Self-denial

The amount given by the widow is described as two copper coins. These coins were called leptas, and equaled 1/64th of a day's wage. Combined, these two coins had a value of one-fourth of a penny! They were the smallest coins in existence.

In the preface to this passage, Jesus had finished a discourse and was sitting within view of the outer portion of the temple known as the women's court. In the women's court were thirteen trumpet-shaped metal chests in which to drop offerings. Each chest was for a different purpose. Some held the money for temple tribute, others for sacrifices, or wood, or other temple necessities. As Jesus watched, a number of wealthy people were coming and dropping large sums into the chests. Their contributions were hard to ignore as the metallic money struck the metal chests. The givers didn't need a press conference to announce their donations—the sound of the clinking coins was sufficient in getting one's attention. In contrast, the widow's coins were the thinnest of all, and would hardly make a sound.

It was easy to be impressed by the generous offerings being made by those who were well off, and Jesus did not condemn them. Those who have much should give much. But Jesus was not as impressed with the total given as He was with the proportion of the widow's gift. They gave a contribution. She made a sacrifice.

Surplus giving vs. sacrificial giving

This is Jesus' point. All the other contributors were making donations. She was making a true sacrifice. Her outlook was dramatically altered in every way because of the scope of her gift. As one commentator wrote, "Few practice self-denial for the practice of charity."[2] He didn't

---

[2]*Barnes Notes, The Commentary of Mark,* by Albert Barnes, p. 377.

say few practice charity, he said few practice self-denial for the practice of charity. While Ted Turner gave away a billion dollars—a tremendous gift—he still has billions and billions left. It was a wonderful contribution, but it can hardly be considered a sacrifice. He still lives in splendor, unaffected by his generosity.

Webster's defines self-denial as "a restraint or limitation of one's own desires or interests, a refusal to satisfy a request or desire." The difference between the rich contributors and the widow was that "they put in out of their surplus." Webster's defines surplus as "the amount that remains when use, or need is satisfied" (emphasis added). After these wealthy givers had taken care of all their needs and wants, they still had more. They didn't even give their entire surplus, but "out of" their surplus. They had money left over beyond their wants and needs. Jesus raised the standard of giving to a new height, and highlighted a virtue of true generosity: self-denial.

Jesus showed us what God considers to be noteworthy in our giving. Our self-denial far outweighs the number of zeroes that might accompany any financial gift we might make. Regardless, the size of our gift to God is of no consequence to Him, because no one can give to God anything that doesn't already belong to Him. The act of giving was never designed to fill God's coffers. It was designed to remind us that everything we receive is from God and that He will provide for us.

As David said when he was gathering contributions to build God's temple: "Both riches and honor come from You, and You rule over all, and in Your hand is power and might; and it lies in Your hand to make great, and to strengthen everyone. Now therefore, our God, we thank You, and praise Your glorious name. But who am I and who are my people that we should be able to offer as generously as this? For all things come from You, and from Your hand we have given You" (1 Chronicles 29:12–14). Again, in Haggai 2:8 we read "'The silver is Mine, and the gold is Mine,' declares the Lord of hosts."

The widow's example causes us to ask ourselves whether the virtue of self-denial is present in our giving. It is possible to impress people with the size of our gifts to Christ, to His church, and to His ministry. Yet, if we are giving only out of our surplus with no evidence of self-denial, heaven yawns.

We need to ask ourselves what comfort or convenience we are willing to put on the block for Jesus' sake? Soren Kierkegaard said, "One single act performed with true self-denial, in renunciation of the world, is infinitely more of a revival and more of Christianity than 1,000 or 10,000 or 100,000 or 1,000,000 persons, so long as they keep it ambiguous." When we are willing to develop the virtue of self-denial, we are well on our way to a wonderful defining moment.

The next virtue evident in the widow's act of generosity is:

Faith

On the face of it, this story may seem to be about money, but it isn't. It's about faith. This poor widow put in all she had to live on! She could do so because she had faith that God would not leave her destitute. He would provide for her.

She wasn't playing a heavenly slot-game with God, the way some Christians do. Their thinking is, "If I put in a quarter, I can sit back and watch as God gives me $100." No, the widow offered to God all she had to live on because she knew that God would provide her food, shelter, and clothing.

What role does faith play in our own giving? If we give only what we can "afford," what does that mean? Often what we can afford is simply what is left over after we have paid for all the things we want. This kind of giving demonstrates no faith at all and has little value in God's eyes, whether we give one dollar or one billion dollars.

One of our greatest fears is that our needs will not be met. We worry that one day we will be unable to provide the necessities of life for ourselves. The widow displayed far more than mere generosity—she was making an incredible statement about her ability to trust in God. How had God met her needs in the past? What memories of His faithful provision for her allowed her mind and heart to be at peace in relinquishing the only form of financial security she possessed? Don't be deceived—this act wasn't just some ill-considered spontaneous act she would later regret—there was a history behind this act.

Each of us has a history with God. We can all point to times when we have needed Him to provide something specific for us—and He has! As the years go by, and our mental scrapbook begins to fill up with more and more examples of God's faithfulness. Our faith in Him grows, and our fears of being left high and dry by God recede.

Most of us need a financial safety net, yet this widow knew she had something more dependable than a pension, or mutual fund, or Social Security; she had a heavenly Father who watched over her tenderly. And while saving for the future is prudent and good biblical advice, savings can be lost, stolen, or taken from us. To put your faith in these things is foolish. Money belongs in the bank, but faith belongs in God, and Him alone.

There was a time when polio was a real threat. People lived in fear of the disease. Many children died, and many more were disabled. Finally, a vaccine was discovered by Dr. Jonas Salk. His faith in the vaccine was tested in one symbolic act. When he was sure his vaccine would work, he gave it first to himself, and then to his wife and three little sons. If the vaccine did not work, he and his family could contract polio. But it was successful and has saved countless lives.[3]

Dr. Salk was willing to take such a great risk because of his faith in his vaccine. The widow was willing to give everything she had because of her faith in God's providence. She knew He would never forsake or desert her. She knew He would provide her food, shelter, and clothing.

How many of our financial decisions are based on the financial virtue of faith in God?

[3]*American Heroes of the 20th Century*, Harold and Doris Faber, (New York: Random House, 1967), p. 135.

But while faith is a sterling financial virtue, destined to provide us a wonderful defining moment, there is another financial virtue we often fail to recognize, and that is:

Love

Self-denial goes hand-in-hand with love. As a husband and a father, I am willing to go without many things to ensure that my wife and children have all they need. I feel no resentment in this. Such sacrifice is a pleasure and a joy. My love for my family is greater than all my own needs.

But what would lead a destitute widow to give an offering of the last scrap of money she had? She wasn't doing it for show—no one but Jesus took notice. She did it out of love!

We are observing an earthshaking moment here. This woman was completely impoverished. Yet her love for God was so real and her faith in God so strong that she gave everything she had to Him.

Imagine if we could hear her testimony. Her walk with God must have been amazing—full of blessings and God's provision for her! That is why she felt no danger about giving away all she had in her most vulnerable moment. How many times before had God met her needs? How often had He provided for her in a way so wonderful that she could come to the place where she had more faith in God than in money? Her act of total sacrifice was an act of pure love for God.

No wonder Jesus called His disciples together to witness this woman's defining moment. Rarely is so deep a love, so vibrant a faith, demonstrated. We don't read that Jesus ever sought to gain her attention, so it appears she was never made aware that anyone had noticed her. But God noticed.

We must ask ourselves what the place of love is in our own giving? When we love someone, really love them, we desire to be extravagant in our demonstrations of love. Jesus reminded the disciples that she had given all. Her tremendous sacrifice was part of the gift.

In John 12:3–5 we read the story of Mary (the sister of Martha) and her costly gift. "Mary therefore took a pound of very costly perfume

of pure nard, and anointed the feet of Jesus, and wiped His feet with her hair; and the house was filled with the fragrance of the perfume. But Judas Iscariot, one of His disciples, who was intending to betray Him, said, 'Why was this perfume not sold for three hundred denarii, and given to poor people?'" Judas didn't understand that the cost of the perfume was part of the gift of love.

How many of our financial decisions have been motivated by our love of God and nothing else? This is a question we must consider deeply. We may have been generous, but what really motivated the generosity? True love is an expensive gift, because it involves giving more than money—it involves giving compassion and adoration as an integral part of every gift you give. Had this woman's gift been bereft of love, it would have drawn the same heavenly attention as all the other gifts given that day. I have received very expensive gifts in my life, but my most cherished gifts are those simple, inexpensive gifts, with little or no monetary value, but dripping with real love.

Some of our defining moments are lived out in view of heaven alone. Yet they are just as important as defining moments the whole world sees. But beyond all these wonderful virtues remains one more:

Secrecy

Sometimes our defining moments come and we don't even realize it. *The Truman Show* fascinated me. A man named Truman was chosen from birth to have his life become a TV show for millions of viewers to enjoy. He believed he was living a normal life. Yet everything in his life was carefully choreographed without his knowledge. He lived his entire life within the confines of a huge movie stage.

In a way, we are all in the same boat. At times we are on center stage and everyone is watching, yet we don't have a clue. People are watching our lives to see how we will respond in a given situation.

Jesus soundly criticized the Pharisees who made a great show of spirituality and called attention to themselves, but who privately were hypocrites. Yet here He called not only the disciples to witness the widow's generous act, but history and every future disciple of His!

Chances are the widow died without knowing how proud Jesus was of her. While other well-dressed people were ostentatiously dropping their noisy offerings into the trumpet-shaped chests, this old woman came and gently dropped in her last two thin coins. No one heard her coins over the clattering of the other large gifts. She quietly walked away, unaware that her brief moment of secret self-denial, faith, and love would teach millions down through the centuries the meaning and nature of true giving. But how those two tiny coins resounded in heaven!

Paul Tournier wrote, "God calls each of us in secret to make certain sacrifices, which always involve a risk, even though it may differ from person to person. God speaks to the crowd, but His call comes to individuals, and through their personal obedience He acts. He does not promise them success, or even final victory in this life. The goal of the adventure to which He commits them is in heaven. God does not promise that He will protect them from trials, from material cares, from sickness, from physical or moral suffering. He promises only that He will be with them in all these trials, and that He will sustain them if they remain faithful to Him."[4]

Playing to two audiences

One of the best tests of the sincerity and purity of our giving is how much we're willing to keep it a secret. If others find out we've been very generous they will lavish us with praise, kudos, and thanks. This is why financial decisions are such defining moments for us—they can't help but reveal the condition of our heart.

The widow's act reminds us that we have two audiences watching us, this world's, and heaven's. Our gifts can cause a celebration either

---

[4]*Draper's Book of Quotations for the Christian World* (Tyndale House Publishers, Inc., Wheaton, Illinois, 1992), by Edith Draper, #5385.

here, or in heaven, but seldom in both places. Of all the hundreds and thousands of people milling around the temple, this woman's quiet act of love and devotion drew the attention of God.

When I was about 20 years old, I had an apartment in Long Beach, California. I worked full-time at a minimum wage job, and went to school at night at a Bible Institute. Money was always in short supply, with living expenses leaving me with more month than money. There were times when I had a week left to payday and no food. I never told anyone—mostly out of a mixture of pride and shame.

I had grown up in Peninsula Baptist Church in Palos Verdes, and though I had moved out of the area, I still attended faithfully. I never told anyone of my desperate predicament (you know what an appetite a twenty-year-old has!), yet several times, after an evening service, I would walk back to my '69 Volkswagen Beetle and find the car filled to the brim with groceries. To this day, I have never found out who did it. They wanted it kept a secret, but heaven saw, and rejoiced with me!

The four financial virtues: self-denial, faith, love, and secrecy. Are these the virtues you are cultivating in your financial decisions? Alan Cole, in his commentary on the widow's gift, writes, "In days when Christian churches are dazzled by large incomes and ambitious blueprints, it is well to remember that the Lord measures giving not by what we give, but by what we keep for ourselves; and the widow kept nothing, but gave all."[5]

The widow was defined by these four financial virtues. So will we. Remember, defining moments are not the result of out-of-character reactions. Rather, they are the climax of ingrained attitudes. Defining moments spring out of our living habits.

For each of us, a financially defining moment will come our way. Are we preparing for a moment that will make heaven take notice, even if no one else ever sees?

---

[5] *The Tyndale Commentary Series, The Book of Mark*, by Alan Cole, p. 196.

DISCUSSION QUESTIONS

Read Mark 12:41–44 and Luke 21:1–4

1. How can the way we spend our money help to define us?

2. Can you name one financial expenditure you have made that you feel defined you in a positive way spiritually? In a negative way?

3. What comfort or convenience would you be willing to give up for the sake of Christ, and why does this question sound so foreign to us?

4. How could we practice self-denial in our financial matters without ending up giving away everything we have? How do we find balance without ignoring the issue of self-denial?

5. What would you say is the place of faith in your financial giving and spending? How does it show itself?

6. If God doesn't need our money, why do you think He asks us to give it to Him?

7. Give some examples of how God has met your financial needs in the past. How does that history with God affect your present financial decisions?

8. Often we make financial decisions based solely on how much money we have, but how much should our love of Christ affect those decisions? How is our love for Christ affecting our own giving?

9. Can you recount a time when you were able to help minister to someone financially, but secretly? Why did you do this, and how did you feel afterward?

Personal Reflection

We live our lives constantly before two audiences, this world and heaven. The simple fact is that each of our hearts are attached to our treasures, and therefore our spending is not only a financial, but a spiritual issue. Our checkbooks are perhaps a deeper insight to our souls than our prayer journals.

Follow-through

List the three biggest financial expenditures you have made recently, and the next several you are contemplating. Then run them through the grid of self-denial, faith, love, and secrecy. Take some time and ask yourself the hard question: how much is enough for me? Ask God what He would want you to do for Him with the finances He's entrusted to you.

THE STORY OF MARK

When he realized this, he went to the house of Mary, the mother of John who was also called Mark, where many were gathered together and were praying.

Acts 12:12

When they reached Salamis, they began to proclaim the word of God in the synagogues of the Jews; and they also had John as their helper.

Acts 13:5

Paul and his companions put out to sea from Paphos and came to Perga in Pamphylia; and John left them and returned to Jerusalem.

Acts 13:13

After some days Paul said to Barnabas, "Let us return and visit the brethren in every city in which we proclaimed the word of the Lord, and see how they are." And Barnabas was desirous of taking John, called Mark, along with them also. But Paul kept insisting that they should not take him along who had deserted them in Pamphylia and had not gone with them to the work. And there arose such a sharp disagreement that they separated from one another, and Barnabas took Mark with him and sailed away to Cyprus. But Paul chose Silas and departed, being committed by the brethren to the grace of the Lord.

Acts 15:36–40

Chapter Eleven

PROMISES FOR RENT: DECISIONS OF DESERTION

One of the blackest words we can ever use against someone is deserter. Few words arouse such anger and disgust among people. In battle, awards are given to those who fight and die valiantly. But punishments are meted out to those who desert. In many armies desertion is a capital offense.

Webster's defines desertion as "the abandonment without consent or legal justification of a person, post, or relationship and the associated duties and obligations. A state of being deserted or forsaken." We have often heard it said, "No one likes a quitter." In this politically-correct age, that motto has withstood public scrutiny; we still don't like quitters. You can be immoral, dishonest, and even violent, and we can forgive you, but we still don't like quitters.

I love the story about the high school basketball coach who was attempting to motivate his players to persevere through a difficult season. Halfway through the season he stood before the team and said, "Did Michael Jordan ever quit?" The team responded, "No!"

He yelled, "What about the Wright brothers? Did they ever give up?"

"No!" hollered back the team.

"Did Muhammad Ali ever quit?" Again, the team yelled, "No!"

"Did Elmer McAllister ever quit?" There was a long silence.

Finally, one player was bold enough to ask, "Who's Elmer McAllister? We never heard of him."

The coach snapped back, "Of course you never heard of him—he quit!"[1]

In this chapter, we examine the life of a man who rubbed elbows and traveled with such luminaries as Paul the apostle and Barnabas. In fact, he was in such favor with Paul and Barnabas that he was invited to come help them on a missionary tour, a great honor. In exactly what way he was to help, we do not know, but since the trip would be dangerous and difficult, his part must have been important.

His name is John Mark, or Mark, as he is commonly known. He first appears in Acts 12:12, where we read that "[Peter came] to the house of Mary, the mother of John who was also called Mark, where many were gathered together and were praying." Then we see John Mark begin to become more prominent, mentioned as a companion to Paul and Barnabas. "When they reached Salamis, they began to proclaim the word of God in the synagogues of the Jews; and they also had John as their helper" (Acts 13:5). Finally we read, "Now Paul and his companions put out to sea from Paphos and came to Perga in Pamphylia; and John left them and returned to Jerusalem" (Acts 13:13).

If this were all the information we had, we would assume that there was a good reason for his departure. But in Acts 15:36–40 we find out

---

[1] *Orange County Register*, Business: "Success means never having to say I quit," by Harvey MacKay, 5/4/98.

what really happened. "And after some days Paul said to Barnabas, 'Let us return and visit the brethren in every city in which we proclaimed the word of the Lord, and see how they are.'" And Barnabas was desirous of taking John, called Mark, along with them also. But Paul kept insisting that they should not take him along who had deserted them in Pamphylia and had not gone with them to the work. And there arose such a sharp disagreement that they separated from one another, and Barnabas took Mark with him and sailed away to Cyprus. But Paul chose Silas and departed, being committed by the brethren to the grace of the Lord."

John Mark quit. He deserted.

Sooner or later, each of us will be tempted to desert our post. It might be a spiritual desertion, a relational desertion, or a responsibility desertion. How do we keep ourselves from making the same mistake as Mark? Let's begin by chronicling the anatomy of his desertion. First, we must recognize that:

The reason for the desertion isn't always apparent

Conspicuously missing from the account in Acts is the reason Mark left. Many scholars have conjectured one reason or another, but we don't know for certain. All we can glean is that there was no legitimate excuse for Mark to leave. If there had been, the issue would not have grown so hot between Paul and Barnabas. What was clear is that when Paul and Barnabas really needed him, Mark was a no-show.

The reasons we quit aren't always immediately apparent. We often decide to quit out of frustration, without honestly reviewing our feelings. The pressures of life and ministry at any level—Sunday school teacher, helper, elder, pastor, teacher, parent, spouse, boss, child—can seem overwhelming.

Years ago the pressures of pastoral ministry were swamping me, and I grew discouraged. I wanted to quit. I was not very objective about it. I did not want to be honest with myself because I was afraid I might not

like what I would discover. Besides, I had made up my mind to quit, and having resolved to do so made me feel better.

I had given it my all, working 70–80 hour weeks for years. Before I became a pastor, I had to work two or three jobs at a time with few vacations. When I became a pastor, I never slowed down. Sure enough, I hit the wall. It took some self-honesty before I could admit that I had put the wall there. In everything we do, our ego and self-centeredness creep in, even in ministry—especially in ministry.

I had never noticed how a desire for notoriety and recognition had begun to drive me. Outwardly, I was doing ministry, but from God's perspective, I was building the Dan Schaeffer empire. I believe that is the explanation for much of all that is called "burnout" among Christian workers. But Jesus didn't place that burden on me, He came to remove it (Matthew 11:28–30).

I identify with Mark. At the point of his desertion, he needed to go in for servicing. Like our old minivan's transmission, Mark could not stay in gear. He kept slipping out, and that ruined the ride for all three of them.

The reason for a desertion is not always apparent. But the reason may be that:

Our original motivation has cooled

How often it happens that, like John Mark, someone wants to become involved in a ministry, undertaking, or relationship. Initially, they do a great job, but after awhile the excitement wears off. The commitment enters a difficult, arduous, even grueling stage. The novelty has worn off. The fun is gone.

Imagine the send-off the church must have given to Paul, Barnabas, and John Mark as they set out on that important missionary journey. How excited and motivated Mark must have been! But his motivation may not have been pure, and an impure motivation will wane.

When we make a promise, we are assuring someone that they can trust us, that we will deliver the goods. A promise can take the form of vows at a wedding, a signature on a contract, the credit card we sign up for and promise to repay, or just simply doing what we've promised we would. The problem is that we often feel one way when making the promise, and completely another when the bill for our commitment comes due. How often have we promised to help someone fix their car, or clean their house without thinking about the cost? One day, when they are in need, they will ask us to help. And it will come at the worst possible time.

It is a given that we will sometimes be overworked, overscheduled, and exhausted. But there is our promise being handed back to us, and someone asking what our promise is worth. The easiest thing to do is make an excuse, to beg off. This serves to help retain our reputation, as well as get us off the hook. But each time we do so, our character is damaged, and we soon become more prone to escape commitment than keep it. We become better and better liars as our character slowly erodes. But the worst lie is the one we have to swallow ourselves, believing that we are really the people we pretend to be.

Once the backslaps and attaboys have stopped coming, once the band stops playing and the confetti stops falling, we begin to feel more like Don Quixote tilting at windmills than the knight-in-shining-armor. When we are alone, and nobody knows or even cares what we're doing, we ask ourselves, "Why am I doing this?" If we do not come up with the right answer, we are a likely candidate to go AWOL (absent without leave). How many projects, relationships, or commitments have you deserted? Often, the reason can be traced to a motivation that is so weak the least bit of adversity causes us to abdicate our responsibilities.

Keeping our faces to the coal

During World War II, England needed to increase its production of coal. Winston Churchill called labor leaders together to enlist their support. As he concluded his presentation he asked them to picture a parade in Piccadilly Circus after the war. First would come the sailors

who kept the vital sea-lanes open. Then would come the soldiers who had returned home from Dunkirk and then gone on to defeat Rommel in Africa. Then would come the pilots who had driven the Luftwaffe from the sky. Last of all, said Churchill, would come a long line of sweat-stained, soot-streaked men in miner's caps. Someone would cry from the crowd, "And where were you during the critical days of our struggle?" And from 10,000 throats would come the answer, "We were deep in the earth with our faces to the coal."

So what will keep our faces to the coal of hardship and difficulty? What will keep us from going AWOL in a difficult ministry, marriage, project, friendship, or commitment? I have discovered only one thing. It is found in 2 Corinthians 5:14: "The love of Christ controls us, having concluded this, that one died for all, therefore all died."

Why should I be doing any ministry? Because I love Jesus! And this is how I demonstrate it: by using my gifts and talents to accomplish His purpose for me. Why should I remain faithful in my marriage? There are dozens of reasons, but they will all develop leaks save one—because I love Christ. If I do not love Him, everything else becomes a moot point.

That's why Jesus said, in John 14:15, "If you love Me, you will keep My commandments." Why should one remain a faithful friend, or stick with a difficult marriage or situation, or tough it out in a thankless ministry? Because of love for Jesus, that's why.

In your defining moment, when you're tempted to desert, the one thing that will keep you faithful is your love for the One who created you, suffered for you, died for you, was raised for you, and who summons you to a higher calling. Every other motivation runs the risk of leading to desertion.

A third aspect of desertion is that:

Its effects are instantaneous and discouraging

Mark volunteered for this historic and vital mission. He signed up for a big responsibility, knowing full well the trip would be difficult. Paul and

Barnabas took a chance on Mark, but at Perga he let them down. He told them, in essence, "This is as far as I go. I've had it. I'm going home."

How often did Paul and Barnabas feel the loss of Mark? How many times did they wish he was with them to make their journey easier? It's clear that the trip became more difficult because Mark had deserted.

A strange dynamic occurs when one person's excitement begins to fade from a project. Soon others start to wonder why they are still doing it.

Webster's defines a promise as "a pledge to do something." Some might say that promises are just words, and situations change. That is true. Promises are just words, and situations do change. But promises are our words. People expect us to keep them. I have three children who find themselves dinosaurs in their classrooms because their parents aren't divorced. But because we've kept our vows, my children go to bed at night peacefully and wake up without worrying whether daddy and mommy are still going to be married. Every promise we keep sculpts our character into something beautiful. Every promise we break damages it.

Do we realize how important just showing up is? Having worked with volunteers in churches for years, I can tell you what a blessing it is when someone who tells us they are going to do something actually sees the job through to the end. When the excitement is high everyone wants to show up. When things start to get challenging, or drudgery settles in, you find out who's really serious. Are you in that position right now? Are there people depending on you to show up, to be there, to finish what you started in a ministry, a marriage, a family, a project, a relationship? You need to know what a terrible effect desertion has on those around you.

But beyond how our decision will affect others, beware, we won't escape unscathed either. For we will soon discover that:

Our reputation will be adversely affected

Mark must have had a sterling reputation to begin with for Paul and Barnabas to trust him with such an important task and responsibility.

They must have prayed long and hard about this issue, and arrived at the conclusion that no one would be more dependable than young Mark.

When we decide to desert our post, our reputation will immediately be affected. Trust and respect are usually the first things that go.

Dads and moms who desert their post in the family or marriage lose trust and respect. Those involved in various ministries who desert their post lose trust and respect. The price for desertion is high. The greater our promises and responsibilities, the greater the blow to our reputation when we desert them.

If a clerk at Seven-Eleven does not show up to work, the convenience store is going to be shorthanded, and it might take an extra 5 minutes to get your Slushee. On the other hand, if a firefighter or police officer doesn't show up when they are needed, much more is at stake. The anger directed at the firefighter and police officer for not showing will be greater than that shown toward the lazy clerk.

Mark was not along on some sightseeing trip with Paul and Barnabas. He had promised to stay with them and meet a tangible need. When they needed him, he went AWOL.

We must not blame people for withholding trust and respect in these moments. Love should be unconditional, but respect and trust must be earned. Paul never stopped loving or caring for Mark, but for a time he did stop trusting him. He didn't look as highly upon him as he once did. But beyond affecting our reputation, deserting affects others we care for, because:

Desertion drives wedges between us
We know that Barnabas and Mark were cousins. It was only natural that Barnabas, the son of encouragement, would want to give his cousin another chance. The Greek word for "sharp disagreement" is the word *paroxysmos*, from which we get our English word paroxysm. It means a sudden, violent emotion or action, an outburst.

Both Barnabas and Paul were getting steamed up about this issue. Their once great friendship and team was being fractured over this issue. We can ask ourselves why Mark's desertion should drive a wedge between Paul and Barnabas. In actuality, it didn't. The desertion didn't cause the problem, it was the issue of bringing Mark back on the team that caused the problem.

To Barnabas, whatever had happened before was behind them. Mark was different now. To Paul it wasn't. He knew that they were involved in a life-and-death enterprise. At any time severe persecution could arise, or pressures come, and Mark might bail on them again. Paul didn't want to take that risk.

It was Paul who called Mark's actions desertion. Those are strong words for strong feelings. How often do you see someone forced to leave a project that many people are working on, and then discover people taking sides? Parents get divorced, and sons and daughters take different sides, some supporting mom, some dad. When a marriage goes south, in-laws suddenly become outlaws.

Have you considered what your desertion could do to those around you? No matter what you say or how you try to explain it, your desertion drives wedges between you and those closest to you.

But lastly, and most importantly, in the anatomy of a decision to desert it is important to know that there is hope, even if you've failed before:

Our failures need not be permanent

Eventually, Mark proved himself again in ministry. Paul began to trust him more and more. How do we know? In Colossians 4:10, we find Mark again in company with Paul. "Aristarchus, my fellow prisoner, sends you his greetings; and also Barnabas' cousin Mark (about whom you received instructions: if he comes to you, welcome him). Then again, in 2 Timothy we read Paul saying, "Only Luke is with me. Pick up Mark and bring him with you, for he is useful to me for service"

(4:11). Is this the same Mark? Yes! The one Paul accused of deserting him and did not want around anymore? Absolutely the same fellow!

Mark had gone from *persona non grata* to being "useful to me for service." Isn't that great to know? The Word of God is such a book of hope for those who have failed. Somewhere, Mark realized his mistake, reevaluated his behavior, and met up again with Paul. I'm sure there was an apology, maybe even an explanation. But words don't cut it, only actions do. Mark began to prove his worth again to Paul. He convinced Paul that he could be trusted, that he would not desert him again.

Paul's confidence in Mark grew to such an extent that we read in Paul's letter to Philemon 1:23–25, "Epaphras, my fellow prisoner in Christ Jesus, greets you, as do Mark, Aristarchus, Demas, Luke, my fellow workers." From a deserter to a fellow-worker. What a transformation!

Somewhere, out of sight of the Scripture, Mark had another defining moment which reversed Paul's estimation of him. How do you respond when you have failed someone? When you have deserted a project, a relationship, a commitment, what do you do? Some attempt to explain it away, to justify it—but not those who care about the reputation of Christ and their own character.

Repairing a reputation

In his book written with Ken Blanchard, *Everyone's a Coach*, Don Shula, former head coach of the Miami Dolphins, tells of losing his temper near an open microphone during a televised game with the Los Angeles Rams. Millions of viewers were surprised and shocked by Shula's explicit profanity. Letters soon arrived from all over the country, voicing the disappointment of many who had respected the coach for his integrity. Shula could have given excuses, but he didn't. Everyone who included a return address received a personal apology. He closed each letter by stating, "I value your respect, and will do my best to earn it again."

Of course, we can never undo what we have done—that's history. But the future is a blank page. If we have deserted, we need to get honest with ourselves and admit it. We'll make no progress until we've done this. Then, like Shula, we have a lot of work to do. It is unreasonable to expect people to look at us differently just because we want them to.

Respect is earned, and we must be twice as trustworthy and reliable as we were untrustworthy and unreliable. We must accept the fact that our initial attempts at restoring people's faith in us will be received with skepticism. There will be many doubters, like Paul, but surely there will also be some Barnabases.

As Helen Keller once said, "Character cannot be developed in ease and quiet. Only through experience of trial and suffering can the soul be strengthened, vision cleared, ambition inspired, and success achieved."

It will be hard at times, and you will be tempted to quit—don't! Your character is worth all the effort, and that is what you will be building. I agree with Chuck Swindoll, "It is never too late to start doing what is right."

We live in an age in which words are cheap, and promises are for rent. One of the great new rights of our culture is the right to renege on what we have committed to do. But we live and operate in a new kingdom, the kingdom of God.

Deep down inside we all want to be people of sterling character. Unfortunately, character is expensive; it costs, always. But the benefits of character outweigh the costs. You can sleep nights, and wake up grateful to see the person who looks back at you in the mirror. You no longer have to lie to others or yourself. You become the one person out of a hundred that people can truly count on. Most important, you will not have to play all kinds of mind games to raise your self-esteem, because you will have a legitimate reason to feel good about yourself.

Character may not make you a million dollars or put you on the cover of *People* magazine, but it pays off! Regardless of what we have done before, the promise of character is what we can still become.

DISCUSSION QUESTIONS

Read Acts 12:12; 13:5, 13; 15:36–40

1. Can you recall a time when you deserted Christ or His calling? If you can do so, share this for the encouragement of others.

2. If you were to give a reason for your defection at the moment you defected, what would it be?

3. In hindsight, what do you feel was the real reason for your defection?

4. Impure motives will develop leaks, which lead to discouragement and even desertion of a calling, task, or project. What are some impure motivations that could prompt someone to enlist in a good spiritual calling or task?

5. Have you ever made a promise to someone that you later regretted? What was it, and why did you later regret it?

6. "Every promise we keep sculpts our character into something beautiful, every promise we break damages it." Using this analogy, finish this sentence: "As a result of my track record, my character looks like _____."

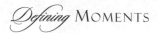

7. Have you ever seen someone's broken promise have repercussions on other people's relationships, like Paul and Barnabas'? What did you learn, and how has this affected you?

8. How hard has it been for you to repair a relationship affected by a broken promise? Have you attempted to repair it, or have you given it up as lost?

Personal Reflection

People take your words, promises, and commitments seriously. This is especially true of children. You can always explain why you are deserting or abandoning your promise, but people don't forget, and regardless of what they may say, they seldom really understand. Transformation into the image of Christ involves becoming more like Him. And He never broke a promise.

Follow-through

Take some time and write down the last five to ten promises you remember making to your family, parents, children, friends, bosses, employees, church, or club. Then resolve that if it is humanly possible, you will keep them all. Rearrange your schedule, inconvenience yourself if necessary. Then, be very careful about any new vows, promises, or commitments you make. Resolve to make new commitments a matter of much prayer.

Conclusion

THE MOST
DEFINING MOMENT

We have studied eleven instances of people learning from their mistakes and successes. God left us these examples and many, many more so that we would not be at a loss to prepare for our greatest defining moment. There are far more stories waiting for you to discover in God's Word, far more examples of warning, and also of faithfulness. The stories of David, Daniel, Elijah, Abraham, Sarah, and countless others wait only to be explored and mined for their valuable treasures of wisdom and insight.

But, hopefully, there is enough here to prepare you for your next defining moment. For in the last analysis, it is your defining moment that is most important. In all these chapters, I have omitted the most important defining-moment decision any person can ever make. I include it here now because I fear to presume that all who read this book may have made this decision.

To be successful in life's decisions but then miss out on eternity would be the ultimate in irony, and the most tragic of all defining moments.

The most defining moment in anyone's life is the decision to surrender to God by accepting Jesus Christ as personal Savior. God's Word, the Bible, tells us that our greatest need is not simply guidance in life, it is a relationship with God. We may have this relationship through Jesus Christ. The result is peace with our heavenly Father, and the gift of eternal life with Him.

If you have never taken this step of faith, remember that faith is not something you wait for like a letter in the mail. Rather, faith is something you step out on, like a bridge over a raging river. Jesus Christ paid the penalty for our sins by dying on the cross. After three days, He rose from the dead, and is now preparing a place for those who put their faith in Him.

If you place your faith in Jesus Christ, you will become a child of the living God and an heir of eternal life. A suggested prayer is included here:

> "Dear Lord, I believe that Jesus is the Son of God. I believe that He came and died to pay the penalty for the sins I have committed. I ask You to forgive me, and to give me the free gift of eternal life that You promised. Come into my life, and cause me to be born again. Amen."

If you prayed this prayer, we encourage you to contact Discovery House Publishing at the address on page 185. They will be happy to send you materials to help you grow in this new relationship with God.

May this be your eternally defining moment.

Note to the Reader

The publisher invites you to share your response to the message of this book by writing Discovery House Publishers, P. O. Box 3566, Grand Rapids, MI 49501, USA or by calling 1-800-653-8333. For information about other Discovery House publications, contact us at the same address and phone number. Find us on the Internet at *http://www.dhp.org/* or send e-mail to *books@dhp.org*.